The Women's Book of Movie Quotes

★ ★ ★

The Women's Book of Movie Quotes

★ ★ ★

Compiled and edited by

JEFF BLOCH

A CITADEL PRESS BOOK

Published by Carol Publishing Group

Copyright © 1993 by Jeff Bloch

Originally published as *Frankly, My Dear*

A Citadel Press Book
Published by Carol Publishing Group
Citadel Press is a registered trademark of Carol Communications, Inc.

Editorial Offices: 600 Madison Avenue, New York, N.Y. 10022
Sales & Distribution Offices: 120 Enterprise Avenue, Secaucus, N.J. 07094
In Canada: Canadian Manda Group, One Atlantic Avenue, Suite 105, Toronto,
    Ontario M6K 3E7
Queries regarding rights and permissions should be addressed to
    Carol Publishing Group, 600 Madison Avenue, New York, N.Y. 10022

Carol Publishing Group books are available at special discounts
for bulk purchases, for sales promotions, fund-raising, or
educational purposes. Special editions can be created to
specifications. For details contact: Special Sales Department,
Carol Publishing Group, 120 Enterprise Avenue, Secaucus, N.J. 07094

Manufactured in the United States of America

10 9 8 7 6 5 4 3 2 1

Library of Congress Cataloging-in-Publication Data

The women's book of movie quotes / compiled and edited by Jeff Bloch.
        p.   cm.
    "A Citadel Press book."
    ISBN 0-8065-1629-1 (pbk.)
    1. Motion pictures—Quotations, maxims, etc. 2. Women in motion
    pictures.   I. Bloch, Jeff.
PN1994.9.W66 1995
791.43′75′082—dc20   94-46326
                                                        CIP

Contents

[Contents]

[Contents]

[Contents]

Introduction

"Fasten your seatbelts. It's going to be a bumpy night." Whatever you may have read or heard about the life of Bette Davis, that single line from *All About Eve* tells you everything you need to know about why Davis remained a movie star for more than five decades. Sure, it's a great line. But it was Davis' delivery—the sassy, unflinching, eager-to-do-battle way she said it—that made the words immortal. Her films are filled with great lines, as are the films of Katharine Hepburn, Mae West, and Marilyn Monroe, and, more recently, those of Meryl Streep, Susan Sarandon, Shirley MacLaine, and Bette Midler. Their words were written well, but these women breathe, spit, and purr life into them on the screen.

The Women's Book of Movie Quotes is a celebration of women in their best moments in the movies—their brilliance, their wit, their guts and passion, their sadness, and even their tragedy. What these women did off-camera may be of interest to their fans, but what they said on the screen should captivate anyone who loves a candid remark, a shocking comeback, or a good joke. Their private lives eventually will fade from memory, but what made them movie stars will live on as long as we watch movies. Gloria Swanson's complaints in *Sunset Boulevard* notwithstanding, all of that "talk, talk, talk!" is precisely why we go to the movies—or rent them. These women always know the right thing to say, without having to go home and sleep on it first. They speak the way we'd all speak if we had good writers.

For more than a year, I have spent my evenings watching movies, ranging from 1930s screwball comedies with Jean Harlow to the peak films of the great stars like Barbara Stanwyck and Joan Crawford, the Hepburn-Tracy classics, and the romantic gems of Ingrid Bergman and Audrey Hepburn. Not surprisingly, some of Hollywood's greatest movies—like *Gone With the Wind, All About Eve, The Philadelphia Story,* and, of course, *The Women*—feature some of the best lines. But there are plenty of morsels from recent movies like *Working Girl, Tootsie, Moonstruck* and, that instant classic, *Thelma & Louise.*

What makes a line immortal? It helps if it's spoken by a star. Clearly, the studios often wrote directly for someone like Bette Davis, capturing her cocky screen presence the way they gave Katharine Hepburn eloquent speeches and Marilyn Monroe breathless bombshells. A few writers and directors are particularly represented here, including Joseph L. Mankiewicz (*All About Eve*), Billy Wilder (*Sunset Boulevard, Some Like It Hot*), and, above all, George Cukor, whose vast body of work includes *The Women, Born Yesterday,* and ten films with Hepburn.

By the same token, some women's screen personas don't really fit into a book of one-liners and zingy repartee. Meryl Streep was brilliant in *Sophie's Choice*, but poignant films tend not to be pithy. The same is true of *Julia* and Jane Fonda films in general, for that matter. Both these actresses are represented here by their comedies rather than their Oscar-caliber classics.

There's no question that Hollywood often has stuck women into outdated and offensive stereotypes, as many more learned books have detailed. But at the same time some screen roles have enabled actresses to do and say the kinds of things that real-life women couldn't have done or said without a major struggle—if at all. Katharine Hepburn was a lawyer in *Adam's Rib* long before many women passed the bar. And Mae West (who wrote most of her own best lines) could hardly be called demure and subservient. Rosalind Russell was a hard-bitten reporter in 1940 in *His Girl Friday,* and Jean Arthur was a hard-nosed member of Congress in 1948 in *A Foreign Affair.* Putting women in these "male" roles was, of course, the point of these movies, and the juxtaposition created the sparks for many of the most quotable lines. Another real-life taboo—divorce— was the topic of so much conversation in Hollywood's Golden Era films that I could have called one chapter, "Reno" (instead, refer to Chapter 8).

Relaxing all those taboos has had its down side, though, in that they just don't write euphemisms like they used to. No one these days would say "Cigarette me, big boy," as Ginger Rogers did in *Young Man of Manhattan* in 1930. And Lauren Bacall would probably have to be a lot more explicit today than when she offered Humphrey Bogart whistling instructions in *To Have and Have Not* in 1944 with the sultry line, "You just put your lips together, and blow."

Women traditionally have had fewer opportunities in Hollywood, but when they get the chance for a great role they run with it. Women in the movies can be strong or weak, victims or monsters ("I'm your number-one fan," says Kathy Bates in *Misery*), bitchy or warm, smart or airy, sexy or serious. And they can do it all in the same movie, like Vivien Leigh in

Gone With the Wind, or Elizabeth Taylor in almost any of her best films. Men, on the other hand…well, as Helen Broderick says in *Top Hat,* "The only difference in men is the color of their neckties."

Being a necktie wearer, I'll leave the serious sociological observations to the experts. *The Women's Book of Movie Quotes* is not cross-referenced and alphabetized like *Bartlett's.* Instead, the chapters are loosely defined to cover a wide range of topics, from come-ons to marriage and from mothers to murder. As you browse through, you'll find some of your most cherished lines as well as some surprises that may tempt you to look beyond the "New Releases" shelf the next time you're in a video store. Chances are if you like the lines quoted here, you'll love the rest of the movie.

It takes a lot of people to make a Hollywood classic, including directors, scores of uncredited screenwriters, and even—in the good old days—the infamous studio system. But at the core are the words and the stars who say them. That's why Bette Davis and her film sorority will never die, and that is what this book applauds, celebrates, and presents.

I would like to thank my agent, Ann Rittenberg, for her encouragement—and the idea—and also my editor, Bruce Shostak, for his valuable advice and his patience.

Jeff Bloch
New York, New York
1993

Anybody Got a Match?

Why don't you come up sometime 'n' see me? I'm home every evening.

> —Mae West to Cary Grant in *She Done Him Wrong* (1933)

★

Don't know if I'm going to be able to sleep. Hint, hint.
  —Karen Black to Jack Nicholson in *Five Easy Pieces* (1970)

★

Please baby, please baby, please baby baby baby, please.
  —Spike Lee in *She's Gotta Have It* (1986)

★

Right here. On the Oriental. With all the lights on.
  —Anjelica Huston to Jack Nicholson in *Prizzi's Honor* (1985)

★

You know you don't have to act with me, Steve. You don't have to say anything, and you don't have to do anything. Not a thing. Oh, maybe just whistle. You know how to whistle, don't you, Steve? You just put your lips together, and blow.
  —Lauren Bacall to Humphrey Bogart in *To Have and Have Not* (1944)

★

Cigarette me, big boy.
  —Ginger Rogers in *Young Man of Manhattan* (1930)

★

Shall we have a cigarette on it?
  —Paul Henreid to Bette Davis in *Now, Voyager* (1942)

★

I suppose you know you have a wonderful body. I'd like to do it in clay.

> —Lola Albright to Kirk Douglas in *Champion* (1949)

★

Would you like to peel the tomato?

> —Liza Minnelli in *The Sterile Cuckoo* (1969)

★

If you'll kindly show me to my quarters, Captain, you can lift anchor anytime.

> —Elizabeth Taylor in *Butterfield 8* (1960)

★

How about coming up to my place for a spot of heavy breathing?

> —Walter Matthau to Carol Burnett in *Pete 'n' Tillie* (1972)

★

Would you like a leg or a breast?

> —Grace Kelly, offering some chicken to Cary Grant, in *To Catch a Thief* (1955)

★

Roy, what if I told you that I wasn't really your mother?

> —Anjelica Huston to John Cusack in *The Grifters* (1990)

★

Anybody got a match?
>   —Lauren Bacall's screen-debut line in *To Have and Have Not* (1944)

★

'Twas the night before Christmas and all through the house, not a creature was stirrin'. Nothin'. No action. Dullsville. You married?
>   —Hope Holiday in *The Apartment* (1960)

★

MADELINE KAHN: Will I see you later?

CLEAVON LITTLE: Well, it all depends on how much vitamin E I can get my hands on.

—*Blazing Saddles* (1974)

★

It's been an evening of ups and downs, hasn't it? Care to continue the motion?

—Maggie Smith to Michael Caine in *California Suite* (1978)

★

WILLIAM HURT: I need tending. I need someone to take care of me. Someone to rub my tired muscles, smooth out my sheets.

KATHLEEN TURNER: Get married.

WH: I just need it for tonight.

—*Body Heat* (1981)

★

Oh, I guess this isn't the bathroom, is it?

—Anne Bancroft, bursting into Dustin Hoffman's bedroom, in *The Graduate* (1967)

★

I'd like you to come in 'til I get the lights on.

—Anne Bancroft, trying again, in *The Graduate* (1967)

★

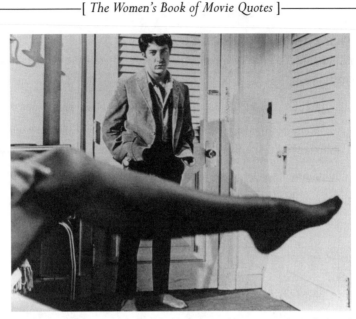

Mrs. Robinson, you're trying to seduce me. Aren't you?
—Dustin Hoffman to Anne Bancroft in *The Graduate*
(1967)

★

ANNE BANCROFT: Do you find me undesirable?
DUSTIN HOFFMAN: Oh no, Mrs. Robinson. I think…I think you're the
most attractive of all my parents' friends. I mean that.
—*The Graduate* (1967)

★

RYAN O'NEAL: Must you stand quite so close?
BARBRA STREISAND: I'm very nearsighted.
    —*What's Up, Doc?* (1972)

★

I am exhausted. Punchy, sick and tired. I can't think and I can't move. I'm just a dead lump of poured-out flesh. Would you like to come up?
    —Holly Hunter to William Hurt in *Broadcast News* (1987)

★

ELLEN BURSTYN: So, wanna fuck?
ALAN ALDA: What?!
EB: You didn't understand the question?
    —*Same Time, Next Year* (1978)

★

HENRY FONDA: Would you care to come in and see Emma?
BARBARA STANWYCK: That's a new one, isn't it?
    —*The Lady Eve* (1941)

★

You know on TV they say you repairmen are a lonely bunch of people. Housewives get lonely, too, although you may not realize it since they haven't made a commercial on the subject.
    —Kathy Baker in *Edward Scissorhands* (1990)

★

I always feel so selfish sleeping alone in a double bed, when there are people in China sleeping on the ground.

—Barbra Streisand to George Segal in *The Owl and the Pussycat* (1970)

★

DUSTIN HOFFMAN: Look, give me your phone number. I'll call you next week.

GIRL: I already gave you my phone number.

DH: Oh, I thought you changed it.

GIRL: Since an hour ago?

—*Tootsie* (1982)

★

Honey, the only question I ever ask any woman is, "What time is your husband coming home?"

—Paul Newman to Patricia Neal in *Hud* (1963)

★

You're not too smart, are you? I like that in a man.

—Kathleen Turner to William Hurt in *Body Heat* (1981)

★

BARBARA STANWYCK: I wonder if I know what you mean.

FRED MACMURRAY: I wonder if you wonder.

—*Double Indemnity* (1944)

★

RICHARD MULLIGAN: Shall we discuss modern architecture?
JOAN HACKETT: It's like talking about current events, or anything, at
the dentist—to delay the drill.
    —*The Group* (1966)

★

Come to my room in a half hour, and bring some rye bread.
    —Jimmy Durante to Mary Wickes in *The Man Who Came to Dinner*
    (1941)

★

Pardon me, ma'am. I'm brand spankin' new in this here town, and I
was hopin' to get a look at the Statue of Liberty.
    —Jon Voight in *Midnight Cowboy* (1969)

★

Do you think that every man who talks to you wants to "establish a
dialogue"? I mean, what do you expect him to do, hang it out of his
trousers and wave it at you?
    —Judith Ivey in *Compromising Positions* (1985)

★

Why don't you slip out of these wet clothes and into a dry martini?
    —Robert Benchley to Ginger Rogers in *The Major and the Minor*
    (1942)

★

You are something we do not have in Russia. That's why I believe in the future of my country.
—Greta Garbo to Melvyn Douglas in *Ninotchka* (1939)

★

RICHARD DREYFUSS: What is it about you that makes a man with a 147-IQ feel like a dribbling idiot?
MARSHA MASON: I don't know. But whatever it is, I thank God for it.
—*The Goodbye Girl* (1977)

★

Wanna dance, or would you rather just suck face?
—Henry Fonda to Katharine Hepburn in *On Golden Pond* (1981)

★

My, you have the busiest hands.
—Una Merkel in *42nd Street* (1933)

★

Will you take your hands off me? What are you playing, osteopath?
—Rosalind Russell to Cary Grant in *His Girl Friday* (1940)

★

The moment I saw you, I had an idea you had an idea.
—Claudette Colbert to Don Ameche in *Midnight* (1939)

★

CLIFF GORMAN: You slumming?
JILL CLAYBURGH: I wasn't up to now.
—*An Unmarried Woman* (1978)

★

PATRICIA NEAL: I was married to Ed for six years. The only thing he
was ever good for was to scratch my back where I couldn't reach it.
PAUL NEWMAN: You still got that itch?
—*Hud* (1963)

★

JESSICA LANGE: See, I figure when you say you want to get to know me better, what you really mean is you want a ten-minute screw in the back of your car.

ED HARRIS: You must think that thing you got between your legs is lined with gold. I can get tail any time I want. I don't have to come crawling after some mean-mouth woman who's got cob-cross ways. Hell, if I just want to bump uglies with somebody, I got plenty of places to go for that.

—*Sweet Dreams* (1985)

★

GRETA GARBO: Must you flirt?

MELVYN DOUGLAS: I don't have to, but I find it natural.

GG: Suppress it.

—*Ninotchka* (1939)

★

ANNETTE BENING: The way you were staring at me, I thought you were going to ask me for something a little more exciting.

WARREN BEATTY: Like what?

AB: Use your imagination.

WB: I'm using it.

AB: Let me know when you're finished.

—*Bugsy* (1991)

★

You're just another good-looking, sweet-talking, charm-oozing, fuck-happy fella with nothing to offer but some dialogue. Dialogue's cheap in Hollywood, Ben. Why don't you run outside and jerk yourself a soda?

—Annette Bening in *Bugsy* (1991)

★

Mr. Allen, this may come as a shock to you, but there are some men who don't end every sentence with a proposition.

—Doris Day to Rock Hudson in *Pillow Talk* (1959)

★

All they have to do is play eight bars of "Come to Me, My Melancholy Baby," and my spine turns to custard. I get goose pimply all over and I come to 'em.

—Marilyn Monroe in *Some Like It Hot* (1959)

★

HELEN JEROME EDDY: Too many girls follow the line of least resistance.
MAE WEST: Yeah, but a good line is hard to resist.

—*Klondike Annie* (1936)

★

The Fairer Sex

Oh, God. Not another fucking beautiful day.
—Sarah Miles in *White Mischief* (1988)

★

MAN: This your girl?
BARBARA STANWYCK: I'm my mother's girl.
—*Golden Boy* (1939)

★

I'm loud and I'm vulgar, and I wear the pants in the house because somebody's got to. But I am not a monster.
—Elizabeth Taylor in *Who's Afraid of Virginia Woolf?* (1966)

★

I don't bray!
—Elizabeth Taylor in *Who's Afraid of Virginia Woolf?* (1966)

★

I don't get tough with anyone, Mr. Gittes. My lawyer does.
—Faye Dunaway in *Chinatown* (1974)

★

Fasten your seat belts. It's going to be a bumpy night.
—Bette Davis in *All About Eve* (1950)

★

There's a name for you ladies, but it isn't used in high society—outside of a kennel.

> —Joan Crawford in *The Women* (1939)

★

EDWARD GARGAN (detective): Just a minute, sister.
JEAN DIXON (maid): If I thought that were true, I'd disown my parents.

> —*My Man Godfrey* (1936)

★

As somebody always said, if you can't say anything nice about anybody, come sit by me.

> —Olympia Dukakis in *Steel Magnolias* (1989)

★

Those women were like animals. I saw this one beautiful handbag that was on sale, but I was too frightened to fight for it. I mean, they were vicious. They kill their own. The woman that finally bought this handbag I know did time.

> —Dustin Hoffman in *Tootsie* (1982)

★

JOAN CRAWFORD: It'll be [sent] out tomorrow, Mrs. Prowler.
ROSALIND RUSSELL: Fowler!

> —*The Women* (1939)

★

I know it's considered noble to accept apologies, but I'm afraid I'm not the noble type.
>   —Joan Crawford in *Female on the Beach* (1955)

★

Helga, I'm not mad at you. I'm mad at the dirt.
>   —Faye Dunaway as Joan Crawford in *Mommie Dearest* (1981)

★

I'm your number-one fan.
>   —Kathy Bates in *Misery* (1990)

★

Let's face it. She's not Mother Teresa. Gandhi would've strangled her.
>   —Judge Reinhold re Bette Midler in *Ruthless People* (1986)

★

If there was an ounce of justice in this world, you wouldn't have come in fifth place. You'd be up on that float in third place.
>   —Mary Steenburgen, consoling Holly Hunter, in *Miss Firecracker* (1989)

★

LITTLE BOY: Cream?
LITTLE GIRL: No, thank you. I take it black—like my men.
>   —*Airplane!* (1980)

★

BUD CORT: You sure have a way with people.
RUTH GORDON: Well, they're my species.
> —*Harold and Maude* (1971)

★

I'm a born defroster.
> —Jessica Lange in *Tootsie* (1982)

★

Just because you have good manners doesn't mean I suddenly turn into Dale Evans.
> —Ellen Burstyn to Kris Kristofferson in *Alice Doesn't Live Here Anymore* (1975)

★

If you don't care what folks says about this family, I does. I has tol' ya and tol' ya that you can always tell a lady by the way she eats in front of folks like a bird, and I ain't aiming for you to go to Mr. John Wilkes's and eat like a field hand and gobble like a hog!
> —Hattie McDaniel to Vivien Leigh in *Gone With the Wind* (1939)

★

If ya throw a lamb chop into a hot oven, what's going to keep it from gettin' done?
> —Joan Crawford in *The Women* (1939)

★

Good morning, ladies and gentlemen, this is a robbery. Now if nobody loses their head, nobody'll lose their head. Simon says y'all lie down on the floor please. Right away. Let's see who'll win a prize for keepin' their cool. Sir, would you do the honors? Take all the cash out of that drawer and put it in a paper bag. You're gonna have an amazing story to tell all your friends. If not, you'll have a tag on your toe. You decide.

—Geena Davis in *Thelma & Louise* (1991)

★

CHRISTINA RICCI: May I have the salt?
ANJELICA HUSTON: What do we say?
CR: Now!

—*The Addams Family* (1991)

★

You eat terrible. You got no manners. Taking your shoes off all the time—that's another thing—and picking your teeth. You're just not couth!

—Judy Holliday to Broderick Crawford in *Born Yesterday* (1950)

★

KATHARINE HEPBURN: I use the right knife and fork. I hope you don't mind.
GINGER ROGERS: All you need's the knife.

—*Stage Door* (1937)

★

Life's a bitch. Now so am I.
—Michelle Pfeiffer in *Batman Returns* (1992)

★

You must have a grip on the saucer that is firm but not obviously so.
The saucer must seem so much a part of your fingers that one would
think it could only be removed by surgery.
—Isabel Jeans to Leslie Caron in *Gigi* (1958)

★

You're having a nervous breakdown. I have those all the time. Just 'cause everything of value in your life has been destroyed, so what? There's still food.

—Glenne Headly in *Making Mr. Right* (1987)

★

In less than two hours, two of them told me that they had had abortions. Three of them told me they were divorced. One of them hasn't talked to her mother in four years. And that one has her little Natalie in a boarding school because she has to travel for her job. I mean, hell, Patsy! Oh, the one with the yeast disease thought she had vaginal herpes. If that's fit conversation for lunch, what's so God-awful terrible about my little tumors?

—Debra Winger in *Terms of Endearment* (1983)

★

There are 108 beads in a Catholic rosary, and there are 108 stitches in a baseball. When I learned that, I gave Jesus a chance.

—Susan Sarandon in *Bull Durham* (1988)

★

RYAN O'NEAL: What are you doing? This is a one-way street!
BARBRA STREISAND: I'm only going one way.

—*What's Up, Doc?* (1972)

★

Peel me a grape.
>—Mae West in *I'm No Angel* (1933)

★

SALLY FIELD: I've come here and said I've sinned and I done wrong and I'm sorry, and I asked for God to forgive me. Now I want to see what this church stands for. I want to see if you'll stand up in that pulpit and say there oughta be justice, there oughta be a union, and if you're smart and you rise up the Lord'll be on your side. And if you don't, then I say there ain't nothin' good for me in that church. And I'm gonna leave it flat.

REVEREND: We're gonna miss your voice in the choir, Norma.

SF: You're gonna hear it raised up someplace else.
>—*Norma Rae* (1979)

★

That's okay, we can walk to the curb from here.
>—Woody Allen, getting out of Diane Keaton's badly parked car, in *Annie Hall* (1977)

★

Gimme an L!! Gimme an I!! Gimme a V!! Gimme an E!! L-I-V-E!! Live!! Otherwise, you got nothing to talk about in the locker room.
>—Ruth Gordon in *Harold and Maude* (1971)

★

I am a descendant, do not forget, of Willie Brodie. He was a man of substance, a cabinetmaker and a designer of gibbets. A member of the town council of Edinburgh, the keeper of two mistresses who bore him five children between them. He played much dice from fighting cocks. Eventually he was a wanted man for having robbed the excise office—not that he needed the money. He was a burglar for the sake of the danger. He died cheerfully on a gibbet of his own devising, in 1788. That is the stuff I am made of.

—Maggie Smith in *The Prime of Miss Jean Brodie* (1969)

★

Oh stewardess, I speak jive.
> —Barbara Billingsley in *Airplane!* (1980)

★

I don't go to church. Kneeling bags my nylons.
> —Jan Sterling in *The Big Carnival* (1951)

★

As long as I know how to get what I want, that's all I wanna know.
> —Judy Holliday in *Born Yesterday* (1950)

★

WILLIAM HOLDEN: Nobody's *born* smart, Billie. You know what the stupidest thing on earth is? An infant.

JUDY HOLLIDAY: What've you got against babies all of a sudden?

WH: Nothing. I've got nothing against a brain that's three-weeks old and empty. But after it hangs around for thirty years and hasn't absorbed anything, I begin to wonder about it.

JH: What makes you think I'm thirty?
> —*Born Yesterday* (1950)

★

Last night I went to bed. I started thinking. I couldn't fall asleep for ten minutes.
> —Judy Holliday in *Born Yesterday* (1950)

★

Whoever opened the window has opened it too wide. Six inches is perfectly adequate. More is vulgar. Forsooth! One should have an innate sense of these things, what is suitable.

—Maggie Smith in *The Prime of Miss Jean Brodie* (1969)

★

I even made poor Louis take me on a Crusade. How's that for blasphemy? I dressed my maids as Amazons and rode bare-breasted halfway to Damascus. Louis had a seizure and I damn near died of windburn. But the troops were dazzled.

—Katharine Hepburn in *The Lion in Winter* (1968)

★

Working Girl

DAVID CLENNON: You want to be Kitty Wells, right?
JESSICA LANGE (as Patsy Cline): Hell no! I want to be Hank Williams!
   —*Sweet Dreams* (1985)

★

Don't fuck with me, fellas! This ain't my first time at the rodeo.
   —Faye Dunaway as Joan Crawford in *Mommie Dearest* (1981)

★

Sorry, gentlemen, to keep you waiting. I'm always late, but I'm worth it.
   —Ann Magnuson in *Making Mr. Right* (1987)

★

I apparently have a masculine temperament. I arouse quickly, consummate prematurely, and I can't wait to get my clothes back on and get out of that bedroom. I seem to be inept at everything—except my work. I'm good at my work. So I confine myself to that. All I want out of life is a 30-share and a 20-rating.
   —Faye Dunaway in *Network* (1976)

★

I'm not sure she's capable of any real feelings. She's television generation. She learned life from Bugs Bunny.

—William Holden re Faye Dunaway in *Network* (1976)

★

I like my convent in Vancouver—out in the woods, wasn't all modern like some of these newfangled convents. We didn't have electricity. Cold water. Bare feet. *Those* were nuns.

—Mary Wickes in *Sister Act* (1992)

★

DANNY DEVITO: What are you, a fucking lawyer?
PENELOPE ANN MILLER: Depends on who I'm with.
   —*Other People's Money* (1991)

★

PETER HACKES (boss): You're just absolutely right and I'm absolutely wrong. It must be nice to always believe you know better, to always think you're the smartest person in the room.
HOLLY HUNTER: No, it's awful.
   —*Broadcast News* (1987)

★

Except for socially, you're my role model.
   —Joan Cusack to Holly Hunter in *Broadcast News* (1987)

★

Never burn bridges. Today's junior prick, tomorrow's senior partner.
   —Sigourney Weaver in *Working Girl* (1988)

★

Oh, okay. I took my life into my own hands. I made a mistake. Fine, I'm sorry, I'll never do it again. I wanna wear my sandals, and I wanna, I wanna go out to lunch. I wanna be normal again!…I don't wanna be in the army!
   —Goldie Hawn in *Private Benjamin* (1980)

★

What's your name, princess?

> —Eileen Brennan to Goldie Hawn in *Private Benjamin* (1980)

★

I became a nurse because all my life, ever since I was a little girl, I was filled with the idea of serving a suffering humanity. After one month with you, Mr. Whiteside, I am going to work in a munitions factory. From now on, anything that I can do to help exterminate the human race will fill me with the greatest of pleasure. Mr. Whiteside, if Florence Nightingale had ever nursed *you*, she would have married Jack the Ripper instead of founding the Red Cross.

> —Mary Wickes to Monty Woolley in *The Man Who Came to Dinner* (1941)

★

BAR OWNER: Would you mind turnin' around for me?

ELLEN BURSTYN: Turn around for you? Why?

BO: I want to look at you.

EB: Well, look at my face. I don't sing with my ass.

> —*Alice Doesn't Live Here Anymore* (1975)

★

Dora, I suspect you're a treasure.

> —Bette Davis to Mary Wickes (nurse) in *Now, Voyager* (1942)

★

Come on, don't go away mad. I didn't buy your proposition; come back with another one. You're an emancipated woman. Learn to lose.
—Danny DeVito in *Other People's Money* (1991)

★

I was gonna go to UCLA, but I couldn't find a place to park.
—Goldie Hawn in *Butterflies Are Free* (1972)

★

Look, I have trouble figuring out the tax on checks. So what! I mean, eight percent is a bitch!
—Teri Garr in *After Hours* (1985)

★

Look, I got a gun out there in my purse. And up to now I've been forgivin' and forgettin' because of the way I was brought up. But I'll tell you one thing. If you ever say another word about me or make another indecent proposal, I'm gonna get that gun of mine, and I'm gonna change you from a rooster to a hen with one shot!
—Dolly Parton, to her boss, Dabney Coleman, in *9 to 5* (1980)

★

He was just made vice president. I have never seen anyone leapfrog so fast to the top in my life—and I have the bad back to prove it.
—Lily Tomlin in *9 to 5* (1980)

★

I have a head for business and a bod for sin. Is there anything wrong with that?
—Melanie Griffith in *Working Girl* (1988)

★

Well, you mustn't think too harshly of my secretaries. They were very kind and understanding when I came to the office after a hard day at home.

> —Claude Rains in *Mr. Skeffington* (1944)

★

They say a moonlit deck is a woman's business office.

> —Barbara Stanwyck in *The Lady Eve* (1941)

★

You know, I spent a lotta years dislikin' women. But I don't dislike you. You're different. You're not a woman. You're more than that. You're a mechanic.

> —Arthur O'Connell in *Operation Petticoat* (1959)

★

JOAN CUSACK: You think anyone who's proud of the work we do is an ass-kisser.

ALBERT BROOKS: No, I think anyone who puckers up their lips and presses it against their boss's buttocks and then smooches is an ass-kisser.

JC: My gosh, for a while there I was attracted to you.

AB: Well, wait a minute, that changes everything!

> —*Broadcast News* (1987)

★

You're going out a youngster, but you've got to come back a star!
—Warner Baxter to Ruby Keeler in *42nd Street* (1933)

★

What you don't like about Miss Dickinson is exactly what I do like about her. She's like a wife, a good wife—devoted, competent. Takes care of everything for me—during the day. Then at night she goes to her home. And I, with no problems and no cares, go to my girl.
—Walter Matthau re Ingrid Bergman in *Cactus Flower* (1969)

★

Diamonds is my career.
—Mae West in *She Done Him Wrong* (1933)

★

Funny business, a woman's career. The things you drop on your way up the ladder so you can move faster, you forget you'll need them again when you get back to being a woman. There's one career all females have in common—whether we like it or not—being a woman. Sooner or later we've got to work at it.
—Bette Davis in *All About Eve* (1950)

★

You don't belong to any man now. You belong to Broadway!
—Adolphe Menjou to Katharine Hepburn in *Morning Glory* (1933)

★

SHIRLEY MACLAINE: You don't remember when Michael
   was choreographing *Anna Karenina*?

ANNE BANCROFT: Yes, of course I do.

SM: And who was he rehearsing for the part of Anna?

AB: You and me.

SM: And...

AB: And—you got pregnant.

SM: And you got nineteen curtain calls.
   —*The Turning Point* (1977)

My first wife was a kindergarten teacher. You know, she got into drugs, and she moved to San Francisco, went into EST, became a moonie. She's with the William Morris Agency now.

—Woody Allen in *Manhattan* (1979)

★

Miss Caswell is an actress, a graduate of the Copacabana School of Dramatic Arts.

—George Sanders re Marilyn Monroe in *All About Eve* (1950)

★

Nobody laughs at me because I laugh first. At me. Me from Seattle. Me with no education. Me with no talent, as you kept reminding me my whole life. Well, Mama, look at me now. I'm a star. Look. Look how I live. Look at my friends. Look where I'm going. I'm not staying in burlesque. I'm moving—maybe up, maybe down—but wherever it is, I'm enjoying it. I'm having the time of my life because, for the first time, it *is* my life. And I love it. I love every second of it.

—Natalie Wood to Rosalind Russell in *Gypsy* (1962)

★

PHILIP COOLIDGE: Your occupation. What do you do?
SUSAN HAYWARD: The best I can.

—*I Want to Live!* (1958)

★

So little. So little, did you say? Why, if there's nothing else, there's applause. I've listened backstage to people applaud. It's like, like waves of love coming over the footlights and wrapping you up. Imagine, to know every night that different hundreds of people love you. They smile, their eyes shine. You've pleased them. They want you. You belong. Just that alone is worth anything.

—Anne Baxter in *All About Eve* (1950)

★

Fashion Statements

Now Steven, I'm perfectly willing to let you tell me how to talk and how to act. But please, don't give me pointers on how to dress. Allow me at least to know more about one thing than you do. After all, I've always been known to have stacks of style.

> —Barbara Stanwyck in *Stella Dallas* (1937)

★

Six thousand dollahs! It's not even leathah!

> —Joan Cusack in *Working Girl* (1988)

★

It's like a circus tent, in mourning for an elephant that died.

> —Jean Arthur, re her own dress, in *A Foreign Affair* (1948)

★

It's marvelous what they can do with man-made fibers these days, isn't it? You'd almost think it was silk—if you weren't familiar with the real thing.

> —Julia McKenzie in *Shirley Valentine* (1989)

★

DOLLY PARTON: You know I'd rather walk on my lips than to criticize anybody, but Janice van Meter, I bet you she's paid five hundred dollars for that dress and don't even bother to wear a girdle.

OLYMPIA DUKAKIS: Looks like two pigs fighting under a blanket.

　　—*Steel Magnolias* (1989)

How did you get into that dress—with a spray gun?
>—Bob Hope to Dorothy Lamour in *Road to Rio* (1948)

★

I have a definite hump on my left shoulder. It cost five hundred pounds and I look like Richard III.
>—Maggie Smith in *California Suite* (1978)

★

That's quite a dress you almost have on.
>—Gene Kelly to Nina Foch in *An American in Paris* (1951)

★

Excuse me, sir, is green the only color these come in?
>—Goldie Hawn, after being issued army fatigues, in *Private Benjamin* (1980)

★

I remember every detail. The Germans wore gray. You wore blue.
>—Humphrey Bogart in *Casablanca* (1942)

★

Sometimes I sing and dance around the house in my underwear. Doesn't make me Madonna. Never will.
>—Joan Cusack in *Working Girl* (1988)

★

Our new one-piece lace foundation garment. Zips up the back and no bones!

>—Judith Allen (model) in *The Women* (1939)

★

RANDOLPH SCOTT: They tell me in Paris if you don't buy your gown from Roberta, you're not dressed at all.

FRED ASTAIRE: I see. Nude if you don't, and nude if you do.

>—*Roberta* (1935)

★

DOLLY PARTON: I haven't left the house without lycra on these thighs since I was fourteen.

OLYMPIA DUKAKIS: You were brought up right.

>—*Steel Magnolias* (1989)

★

I won't have to do with girls who roll up the sleeves of their blouses. We are civilized beings.

>—Maggie Smith in *The Prime of Miss Jean Brodie* (1969)

★

I'll meet you tonight under the moon. Oh, I can see you now—you and the moon. You wear a necktie so I'll know you.

>—Groucho Marx to Margaret Dumont in *The Cocoanuts* (1929)

★

Hysterectomy pants, I call them…
>—Polly Bergen in *Cry-Baby* (1990)

★

Look at her hair! Gosh, I wish mine was that high.
>—Leslie Ann Powers in *Hairspray* (1988)

★

Just hold on, and suck in!
>—Hattie McDaniel, lacing up Vivien Leigh's corset, in
>*Gone With the Wind* (1939)

★

The only thing that separates us from the animals is our ability to accessorize.

> —Olympia Dukakis in *Steel Magnolias* (1989)

★

Oh my God! Someone's been sleeping in my dress!

> —Beatrice Arthur in *Mame* (1974)

★

In my time, women with hair like that didn't come outside in the daylight.

> —Elizabeth Patterson re Mae West in *Go West, Young Man* (1936)

★

BILLY CRYSTAL: That's it? A faceless guy rips off your clothes, and that's the sex fantasy you've been having since you were twelve. Exactly the same?

MEG RYAN: Well, sometimes I vary it a little.

BC: Which part?

MR: What I'm wearing.

> —*When Harry Met Sally...* (1989)

★

If I kept my hair "natural" the way you do, I'd be bald.

> —Rosalind Russell to Coral Browne in *Auntie Mame* (1958)

★

I know exactly how you feel, my dear. The morning after always does looks grim if you happen to be wearing last night's dress.

—Ina Claire to Greta Garbo in *Ninotchka* (1939)

★

Look, Heather left behind one of her Swatches. She'd want you to have it, Veronica. She always said you couldn't accessorize for shit.

—Lisanne Falk in *Heathers* (1989)

★

Here's Looking at You

Good grief! I hate to tell you, dear, but your skin makes the Rocky Mountains look like chiffon velvet!

> —Salon patron, peering through a magnifying lens, in *The Women* (1939)

★

I've aged, Sidney. I'm getting lines in my face. I look like a brand-new, steel-belted radial tire.

> —Maggie Smith in *California Suite* (1978)

★

The cameraman must do luggage commercials. All you could see were the bags under my eyes.

> —Maggie Smith in *California Suite* (1978)

★

I've got to do something about the way I look. I mean, a girl just can't go to Sing-Sing with a green face.

> —Audrey Hepburn in *Breakfast at Tiffany's* (1961)

★

DORIS BLACK (re Dustin Hoffman in drag): I'd like to make her look a little more attractive. How far can you pull back?
CAMERAMAN: How do you feel about Cleveland?
    —*Tootsie* (1982)

★

DIANE LADD: She's from a poor dirt farm.

KEVIN CONWAY (doctor): I find that unbelievable. Aside from her illness at the moment, she is very strong, and a splendid specimen of a young human female—and a comely one. She has the figure of a Venus de Milo. Nope, she definitely got protein somewhere as a child.

   —*Rambling Rose* (1991)

★

Not much meat on her, but what's there is cherce.

   —Spencer Tracy re Katharine Hepburn in *Pat and Mike* (1952)

★

You see, Mr. Scott, in the water I'm a very skinny lady.

   —Shelley Winters in *The Poseidon Adventure* (1972)

★

You don't have to describe Gloria to me, Mr. Liggett. I'd know her with my eyes closed, down in the bottom of a coal mine, during the eclipse of the sun.

   —Tom Ahearne (bartender) re Elizabeth Taylor in *Butterfield 8* (1960)

★

If she were a President, she'd be Babe-raham Lincoln.

   —Dana Carvey in *Wayne's World* (1992)

★

There's nothing to be gained by just looking pretty like Isabella. Every beauty mark must conceal a thought, and every curl be full of humor, as well as brilliantine!

—Merle Oberon in *Wuthering Heights* (1939)

Lady, you certainly don't look like somebody that's just been shipwrecked.

—John Hodiak to Tallulah Bankhead in *Lifeboat* (1944)

★

WILLIAM HOLDEN: What it needs is maybe a little more dialogue.
GLORIA SWANSON: What for? I can say anything I want with my eyes.
  —*Sunset Boulevard* (1950)

★

She's got those eyes that run up and down a man like a searchlight.
  —Dennie Moore re Joan Crawford in *The Women* (1939)

★

Here's looking at you, kid.
  —Humphrey Bogart in *Casablanca* (1942)

★

She came at me in sections. More curves than the scenic railway.
  —Fred Astaire re Cyd Charisse in *The Band Wagon* (1953)

★

You have no idea what a long-legged gal can do without doing anything.
  —Claudette Colbert in *The Palm Beach Story* (1942)

★

With a binding like you've got, people are going to want to know what's in the book.
  —Gene Kelly to Leslie Caron in *An American in Paris* (1951)

★

Pearl, you're curved in the flesh of temptation. Resistance is going to be a darn sight harder for you than for females protected by the shape of sows.

　　—Walter Huston to Jennifer Jones in *Duel in the Sun* (1946)

★

She who is born beautiful is born married.

　　—Marlon Brando in *Viva Zapata!* (1952)

★

ROBERT PRESTON: Wilson, you don't know what it does to a man's ego to be constantly reminded that he's married to a beautiful woman.

JOAN BENNETT: Usually what it does to yours, darling, air does to a balloon.

　　—*The Macomber Affair* (1947)

★

I have this theory that you should be with another person who's just good-looking enough to turn you on. Any excess brings problems. She was much prettier than I needed.

　　—Albert Brooks in *Defending Your Life* (1991)

★

I just haven't got the kind of face that goes with a bankroll.

　　—Thelma Ritter in *Titanic* (1953)

★

I proved, once and for all, that the limb is mightier than the thumb.
    —Claudette Colbert in *It Happened One Night* (1934)

★

Why didn't you take off *all* your clothes? You could have stopped *forty* cars.
        —Clark Gable to Claudette Colbert in *It Happened One Night* (1934)

★

BILLY CRYSTAL: No man can be friends with a woman that he finds attractive. He always wants to have sex with her.

MEG RYAN: So you're saying that a man can be friends with a woman he finds unattractive.

BC: No. You pretty much want to nail them, too.
—*When Harry Met Sally…* (1989)

★

I've gone out with some bums in my day, but they were beautiful. That is the only reason to go out with a bum.
—Mercedes Ruehl in *The Fisher King* (1991)

★

Do you know what I think when I see a pretty girl? Oh, to be eighty again!
—Louis Calhern in *The Magnificent Yankee* (1951)

★

What God has not given to Antoinette Green, Antoinette Green has had done.
—Liza Minnelli in *The Sterile Cuckoo* (1969)

★

You were cute. White, but cute.
—Whoopi Goldberg to Patrick Swayze in *Ghost* (1990)

★

I don't especially like the way I look sometimes, but I never met a man since I was fourteen that didn't want to give me an argument about it.
—Lana Turner in *The Postman Always Rings Twice* (1946)

I notice you don't have any tattoos. I think that's a wise choice. I don't think Jackie Onassis would have gone as far if she'd had an anchor on her arm.

—Steve Martin in *Roxanne* (1987)

★

I never could understand this quaint habit of making a billboard out of one's torso. I must say, however, you've shown the most commendable delicacy in just tattooing the initials and not printing the names, addresses, and telephone numbers.

—Tallulah Bankhead in *Lifeboat* (1944)

★

You look pretty good without your shirt on, you know. The sight of that through the kitchen window made me put down my dishtowel more 'n once.

—Patricia Neal to Paul Newman in *Hud* (1963)

★

MELVYN DOUGLAS: Ninotchka, you like me just a little bit?
GRETA GARBO: Your general appearance is not distasteful.
MD: Thank you.
GG: The whites of your eyes are clear. Your cornea is excellent.

—*Ninotchka* (1939)

★

BILL MURRAY: Well, it works—
DUSTIN HOFFMAN (in drag): But what?
BM: Don't play hard to get.

> —*Tootsie* (1982)

★

Funny thing is, you are sort of attractive, in a corn-fed sort of way. I can imagine some poor girl falling for you if—well, if you threw in a set of dishes.

> —Bette Davis to Richard Travis in *The Man Who Came to Dinner* (1941)

★

He runs four miles a day and has a body like Mark Spitz. Unfortunately, he still has a face like Ernest Borgnine.

> —Ellen Burstyn re her husband in *Same Time, Next Year* (1978)

★

You know, my girlfriends couldn't care if he did triples and landed in a split. They'd just like to see him in his tights.

> —Lisa Lucas re Mikhail Baryshnikov in *The Turning Point* (1977)

★

Michael was not a guy other guys would've made fun of in the locker room, okay?

> —Bette Midler in *Outrageous Fortune* (1987)

★

Did you ever see his feet?

    —Ellen Burstyn in *Alice Doesn't Live Here Anymore* (1975)

★

SHANDRA BERI: He's got a great ass.

DARYL HANNAH: Too bad it's on his shoulders.

    —*Roxanne* (1987)

★

It

Do you think it will ever take the place of night baseball?
> —Deborah Kerr to Cary Grant in *An Affair to Remember* (1957)

★

It's even better when you help.
> —Lauren Bacall to Humphrey Bogart in *To Have and Have Not* (1944)

★

JUDY HOLLIDAY: What are you doin'?
WILLIAM HOLDEN: Well, if you don't know, I must be doing it wrong.
> —*Born Yesterday* (1950)

★

WALTER MATTHAU: I think I'm going to kiss you.
INGRID BERGMAN: When will you know for sure?
> —*Cactus Flower* (1969)

★

I'd love to kiss yuh, but I just washed my hair.
> —Bette Davis in *Cabin in the Cotton* (1932)

★

Was that cannon fire. or is it my heart pounding?
—Ingrid Bergman to Humphrey Bogart in *Casablanca* (1942)

★

I always say a kiss on the hand might feel very good, but a diamond tiara lasts forever.
—Marilyn Monroe in *Gentlemen Prefer Blondes* (1953)

★

I never dreamed that any mere physical experience could be so stimulating.

> —Katharine Hepburn, after surviving the rapids with Humphrey Bogart, in *The African Queen* (1951)

★

Here's a soldier of the South who loves you, Scarlett. Wants to feel your arms around him, wants to carry the memory of your kisses into battle with him. Never mind about loving me. You're a woman who is sending a soldier to his death with a beautiful memory. Scarlett, kiss me. Kiss me, once.

> —Clark Gable to Vivien Leigh in *Gone With the Wind* (1939)

★

If meaningless sex is what you want, why can't you have it with me?

> —Geena Davis in *Earth Girls Are Easy* (1989)

★

I don't understand these modern girls. Well, Polly, for instance—sometimes she won't let you kiss her at all. But there's Cynthia—oh, she'll let you kiss her whenever you want. She doesn't want to swim. She doesn't want to play tennis, go for walks. All she wants to do is kiss you. I'm a nervous wreck!

> —Mickey Rooney in *Love Finds Andy Hardy* (1938)

★

Usually by the time I kiss a guy I already know his mother's maiden name.

   —Goldie Hawn in *Private Benjamin* (1980)

★

Well, it is sort of a favor, isn't it? I mean, when a girl lets you kiss her and, you know, go on from there. Feel her up and, you know, the rest of it, go all the way, and the rest of it. I mean, isn't it a favor? What's in it for her? I mean, she's not getting paid or anything.

   —Art Garfunkel in *Carnal Knowledge* (1971)

★

Schwing!

   —Mike Myers and Dana Carvey in *Wayne's World* (1992)

★

DYAN CANNON: I know that you are in the mood. But honey, I'm not. Now do you want to do it, just like that, with no feeling on my part?
ELLIOTT GOULD: Yeah.

   —*Bob & Carol & Ted & Alice* (1969)

★

First we'll have an orgy, and then we'll go see Tony Bennett.

   —Elliott Gould in *Bob & Carol & Ted & Alice* (1969)

★

TONY CURTIS: It's like smoking without inhaling.
MARILYN MONROE: So inhale.
>   —*Some Like It Hot* (1959)

★

ELIZABETH PERKINS: I mean, I like you and I want to spend the night with you.
TOM HANKS: Do you mean sleep over?
EP: Well, yeah.
TH (referring to bunk beds): Okay. But I get to be on top.
>   —*Big* (1988)

★

I like to watch.
>   —Peter Sellers, meaning television, to Shirley MacLaine, who doesn't, in *Being There* (1979)

★

JACK NICHOLSON: I like the lights on.
SHIRLEY MACLAINE: Then go home and turn them on.
>   —*Terms of Endearment* (1983)

★

What do I do with my other hand?
>   —Art Garfunkel to Candice Bergen in *Carnal Knowledge* (1971)

★

Sometimes when I've got a ballplayer alone, I'll just read Emily Dickinson or Walt Whitman to him. And the guys are so sweet, they always stay and listen. Course, a guy'll listen to anything if he thinks it's foreplay.

>   —Susan Sarandon in *Bull Durham* (1988)

★

Mrs. Robinson, do you think we could say a few words to each other first this time?

>   —Dustin Hoffman to Anne Bancroft in *The Graduate* (1967)

★

I can feel the hot blood pounding through your varicose veins.

>   —Jimmy Durante to Mary Wickes in *The Man Who Came to Dinner* (1941)

★

You have the touch of a love-starved cobra.

>   —Monty Woolley to Mary Wickes in *The Man Who Came to Dinner* (1941)

★

I think we might begin with one or two Latin terms.

>   —John Malkovich, instructing Uma Thurman, in *Dangerous Liaisons* (1988)

★

Is that a ten-gallon hat—or are you just enjoying the show?
—Madeline Kahn in *Blazing Saddles* (1974)

Where do the noses go?
>—Ingrid Bergman to Gary Cooper in *For Whom the Bell Tolls* (1943)

★

Hey, this girl does not have one-night stands. Every guy I have ever slept with—and we are way into double digits here—has come back for more. Every single one!
>—Bette Midler in *Outrageous Fortune* (1987)

★

If I hold you any closer, I'll be in back of you.
>—Groucho Marx to Esther Muir in *A Day at the Races* (1937)

★

Elevate me.
>—Gene Wilder to Teri Garr in *Young Frankenstein* (1974)

★

Here *comes* the bride! Wait, Flap, where'd you learn how to do that?
>—Debra Winger in *Terms of Endearment* (1983)

★

I finally understand what all the fuss is about now. It's just like a whole other ball game.
>—Geena Davis in *Thelma & Louise* (1991)

★

A sculptor friend of Auntie Mame's used this room for about six months. A divine man. Such talented fingers. But oh, what he did to my bust.

—Rosalind Russell in *Auntie Mame* (1958)

★

I haven't had an orgasm like that in nine and a half years. I never thought I was capable of this. I'm ashamed of myself. I am. Glad and ashamed.

—Bette Midler in *Down and Out in Beverly Hills* (1986)

★

If we end up together, then this is the most romantic day of my whole life. And if we don't, then I'm a complete slut.

> —Kathleen Turner to Michael Douglas in *The War of the Roses* (1989)

★

You think you could discreetly move across the hall now?

> —Susan Anspach, after sleeping with Jack Nicholson, in *Five Easy Pieces* (1970)

★

As Balzac said, there goes another novel.

> —Woody Allen in *Annie Hall* (1977)

★

It happens to everyone—men, I mean. We're lucky—women, I mean—we can fake it if we have to.

> —Lesley Ann Warren in *Victor/Victoria* (1982)

★

I thought there'd been an earthquake.

> —Pauline Collins in *Shirley Valentine* (1989)

★

I'll have what she's having.

> —Estelle Reiner to a waiter, observing Meg Ryan mimicking an orgasm, in *When Harry Met Sally…* (1989)

★

It's not the men in my life but the life in my men.
>—Mae West in *I'm No Angel* (1933)

★

JOHN MALKOVICH: You take a long time, by the way.
ANDIE MACDOWELL: Well, it's worth it.
>—*The Object of Beauty* (1991)

★

DEAN BASTOUNES (one-night stand): So what's for breakfast?
ELIZABETH PERKINS: Egg McMuffin. Corner of Broadway and Belmont.
>—*About Last Night…* (1986)

★

Greg, honey, is it supposed to be this soft?
>—Martha Smith in *National Lampoon's Animal House* (1978)

★

Maybe if you didn't call me "ma'am," things might work out better.
>—Brenda Vaccaro to Jon Voight in *Midnight Cowboy* (1969)

★

Why is it that a woman always thinks that the most savage thing she can say to a man is to impugn his cocksmanship?
>—William Holden in *Network* (1976)

★

Dear, what is your first name?

>—Katharine Hepburn to Humphrey Bogart, the morning after, in *The African Queen* (1952)

★

The only people who make love all the time are liars.

>—Louis Jourdan in *Gigi* (1958)

★

Just remember that every relationship starts with a one-night stand.

>—Anthony Edwards in *The Sure Thing* (1985)

★

BILLY CRYSTAL: You meet someone, you have the safe lunch. You decide you like each other enough to move on to dinner. You go dancing, you do the white man's overbite. You go back to her place, you have sex and the minute you're finished, you know what goes through your mind? How long do I have to lie here and hold her before I can get up and go home? Is thirty seconds enough?

MEG RYAN: That's what you're thinking? Is that true?

BC: Sure. All men think that. How long do you like to be held afterwards? All night, right? See, that's the problem. Somewhere between thirty seconds and all night is your problem.

>—*When Harry Met Sally...* (1989)

★

Good morning. Remember me? I'm the fella you slept on last night.
—Clark Gable to Claudette Colbert in *It Happened One Night* (1934)

★

I finally had an orgasm, and my doctor told me it was the wrong kind.
—Tisa Farrow in *Manhattan* (1979)

★

Oh, quit prissin'. I don't think you did it right, anyway.
—Cybill Shepherd to Jeff Bridges in *The Last Picture Show* (1971)

★

Years from now when you talk about this—and you will—be kind.
—Deborah Kerr to John Kerr in *Tea and Sympathy* (1956)

★

DIANE KEATON: It's a dachshund. You know, I mean, it's a penis substitute for me.

WOODY ALLEN: Oh, I would have thought then in your case a Great Dane.
—*Manhattan* (1979)

★

Oh, you men are all alike! Seven or eight quick ones and you're off with the boys, to boast and brag.
—Madeline Kahn in *Young Frankenstein* (1974)

★

L'Amour, L'Amour

L'amour, l'amour. Toujours l'amour!
> —Mary Boland in *The Women* (1939)

★

The thing about love is that you can really make an ass of yourself.
> —Candice Bergen in *Starting Over* (1979)

★

A woman can do anything, get anywhere, as long as she doesn't fall in love.
> —Joan Crawford in *Possessed* (1931)

★

As my old friend Zannebaum used to say, "Women make the best psychoanalysts 'til they fall in love. After that, they make the best patients."
> —Michael Chekhov to Ingrid Bergman in *Spellbound* (1945)

★

I never dated Carlo. I married him. I never dated him.
> —Beatrice Arthur in *Mame* (1974)

★

I refuse to go out with a man whose ass is smaller than mine.
—Elizabeth Perkins in *About Last Night...* (1986)

★

You know this game of love? If you want to take the advice of an old gambler: Some people are lucky at it, some people are jinxed. You shouldn't even sit down at the table.

—Marlene Dietrich to Jean Arthur in *A Foreign Affair* (1948)

I shall die a bachelor.
>—Greta Garbo in *Queen Christina* (1933)

★

Send out for a pizza, rent a film. That's dinner and a movie, and I don't have to deal with some schmuck trying to put his tongue in my ear.
>—Michelle Pfeiffer in *Frankie and Johnny* (1991)

★

I never could understand why it has to be just even—male and female. They're invited for dinner, not for mating.
>—Louise Closser Hale in *Dinner at Eight* (1933)

★

Some minor activity occurs in the medulla and wham, they think they're in love. The next thing they know, they have two children and a canine and then boom, some neuron misfires and they're divorced, miserable, and only get to see their children on Sundays. It is all chemical, Ulysses, and it is all a waste of time.
>—John Malkovich in *Making Mr. Right* (1987)

★

I've been out there dating for twenty years. I've gotten where I can tell in the first fifteen seconds if there's a chance in the world.
>—Mary Kay Place in *The Big Chill* (1983)

★

Well, good night, Michael. It was a wonderful party. My date left with someone else. I had a lot of fun. Do you have any Seconal?

—Teri Garr in *Tootsie* (1982)

★

GLADYS COOPER (mother): And what do you intend to do with your life?

BETTE DAVIS: Get a cat and a parrot and live alone in single blessedness.

—*Now, Voyager* (1942)

★

If there's anything worse than a woman living alone, it's a woman saying she likes it.

—Thelma Ritter to Doris Day in *Pillow Talk* (1959)

★

Men who wear glasses are so much more gentle and sweet and helpless. Haven't you ever noticed it? They get those weak eyes from reading, you know, those long, tiny little columns in the *Wall Street Journal*.

—Marilyn Monroe in *Some Like It Hot* (1959)

★

I don't care how rich he is—as long as he has a yacht, his own private railroad car, and his own toothpaste.

—Marilyn Monroe in *Some Like It Hot* (1959)

★

RALPH BELLAMY (re Cary Grant): He's not the man for you—I can see that—but I sorta like him. He's got a lot of charm.

ROSALIND RUSSELL: Well, he comes by it naturally. His grandfather was a snake.

> —*His Girl Friday* (1940)

★

I won't let myself fall in love with a man who won't trust me no matter what I might do.

> —Marilyn Monroe in *Gentlemen Prefer Blondes* (1953)

★

I like a man who can run faster than I can.

> —Jane Russell in *Gentlemen Prefer Blondes* (1953)

★

HENRY FONDA: What does yours [dream man] look like?

BARBARA STANWYCK: He's a little short guy with lots of money.

HF: Why short?

BS: What does it matter, if he's rich?

> —*The Lady Eve* (1941)

★

No pride at all! That's a luxury a woman in love can't afford.

> —Norma Shearer in *The Women* (1939)

★

JOAN CRAWFORD: Are there books about…good-looking men and cars and things?

SKEETS GALLAGHER: There's always *Dun & Bradstreet*.

  —*Possessed* (1931)

★

You told me that he was good-looking and that he danced beautifully. That's all one is entitled to. You can always read a good book.

  —Phyllis Calvert in *Indiscreet* (1958)

★

MERYL STREEP (re Jack Nicholson): Is he single?

FRIEND: He's famous for it.

  —*Heartburn* (1986)

★

STEVEN HILL (father): Your mother would've loved him.

MERYL STREEP: Yeah. But she was crazy.

  —*Heartburn* (1986)

★

I would never want to belong to any club that would have someone like me for a member. That's the key joke of my adult life, in terms of my relationships with women.

  —Woody Allen in *Annie Hall* (1977)

★

I make it a rule never to get involved with possessed people. [KISS] Actually, it's more of a guideline than a rule.

>   —Bill Murray to Sigourney Weaver in *Ghostbusters*
>   (1984)

★

Always remember two things: I love you—and the name of the bank.
>   —Debbie Reynolds in *The Unsinkable Molly Brown* (1964)

★

You're like an old coat that's hanging in his closet. Every time he reaches in, there you are. Don't be there once.

   —Joan Blondell to Katharine Hepburn in *Desk Set* (1957)

★

They're either married or gay. And if they're not gay, they've just broken up with the most wonderful woman in the world, or they've just broken up with a bitch who looks exactly like me. They're in transition from a monogamous relationship, and they need more space. Or they're tired of space, but they just can't commit. Or they want to commit, but they're afraid to get close. They want to get close, and you don't want to get near them.

   —Mary Kay Place in *The Big Chill* (1983)

★

EDWARD ALBERT: Tell me, Jill, with Ralph is it like the Fourth of July and like Christmas?

GOLDIE HAWN: Not exactly. He has a kind of strength. With him it's more like Labor Day.

   —*Butterflies Are Free* (1972)

★

To the men we have loved! Stinkers.

   —Eve Arden in *Mildred Pierce* (1945)

★

It's the so-called normal guys who always let you down. Sickos never scare me. At least they're committed.

    —Michelle Pfeiffer in *Batman Returns* (1992)

★

I remember in high school her sayin' to me, "Now, what you want to go and sign up for that science class for? There's no girls in that science class. Why don't you take home ec? That's the way to meet the nice boys." I said, "Momma, there ain't no boys in home ec. The boys are in science class."

    —Meryl Streep in *Silkwood* (1983)

★

JILL CLAYBURGH: I understand. It's too much, it's too soon, or you don't like me enough, or you like me too much, or you're frightened or you're guilty, you can't get it up or out or in or what?!
BURT REYNOLDS: That just about covers it.

    —*Starting Over* (1979)

★

Whatever possessed you? You know his religion. How could a girl with a mind of her own have to do with a man who can't think for himself?

    —Maggie Smith in *The Prime of Miss Jean Brodie* (1969)

★

VAN HEFLIN: It's a girder, a molded girder. The army couldn't use it, but a construction engineer'd give his right arm for that.

JOAN CRAWFORD: Why don't you love me like that? I'm much nicer than a girder and a lot more interesting.

—*Possessed* (1947)

★

When men get around me, they get allergic to wedding rings. You know, "Big Sister-type. Good old Ida. You can talk it over with her man-to-man." I'm getting awfully tired of men talking to me man-to-man.

—Eve Arden in *Mildred Pierce* (1945)

★

DANA CARVEY: Wayne, um, what do you do if every time you see this one incredible woman, you think you're gonna hurl?

MIKE MYERS: I say hurl. If you blow chunks and she comes back, she's yours. If you spew and she bolts, it was never meant to be.

—*Wayne's World* (1992)

★

I know, I know. You don't give a hoop what I do. But when I do it you get sore.

—Lauren Bacall to Humphrey Bogart in *To Have and Have Not* (1944)

★

LINDA MILLER: He's nineteen. I know, I know, but he's very mature.
KELLY BISHOP: The problem is, does she fuck him or does she adopt him?

—*An Unmarried Woman* (1978)

★

Look, I'm thirty-five. Does that mean anything to you? Three dash five. When I was in third grade, your mother was pregnant with you. When I graduated from high school, you were suckin' on popsicles. I don't date teenagers.

—Ellen Burstyn in *Alice Doesn't Live Here Anymore* (1975)

★

They're either too young or too old.
They're either too gray or too grassy green.
The pickings are poor and the crop is lean.
There isn't any gravy—the gravy's in the navy.

—Sung by Bette Davis in *Thank Your Lucky Stars* (1943)

★

You have no idea how many women want you when you're getting old. How many liver-spotted female hands reach out to squeeze the last drops from your body, as they go about living longer than we do.

—Richard Whiting in *Starting Over* (1979)

★

She's seventeen. I'm forty-two and she's seventeen. I'm older than her father. Do you believe that? I'm dating a girl wherein I can beat up her father.

—Woody Allen re Mariel Hemingway in *Manhattan* (1979)

★

My relationship with Hal is totally honest. He doesn't tell me he loves me, I don't tell him he's fascinating. It's pure sex.

—Kelly Bishop in *An Unmarried Woman* (1978)

★

OLYMPIA DUKAKIS: Do you love him, Loretta?
CHER: No.
OD: Good. When you love 'em, they drive you crazy, 'cause they know they can.

—*Moonstruck* (1987)

★

MARTHA PLIMPTON: He told me he loved me.
DIANNE WIEST: Aw, sweetie. They say that—then they come.

—*Parenthood* (1989)

★

I wish he'd forget me, but the guy is a memory expert.

—Mae West in *She Done Him Wrong* (1933)

★

WALTER MATTHAU: It's different with a man. When a man is with a younger woman it looks entirely appropriate. But when it's the other way around, it's dis—

INGRID BERGMAN: You go to your church and I'll go to mine.

    —*Cactus Flower* (1969)

★

ALAN BATES: Do you want to see other men?

JILL CLAYBURGH: Not today.

    —*An Unmarried Woman* (1978)

★

Michael, I know there's pain in every relationship. I would just like to have my pain now, okay? I mean, otherwise I'll just wait by the phone, and then if you don't call I'll have pain *and* wait by the phone. It's a waste of time.

    —Teri Garr to Dustin Hoffman in *Tootsie* (1982)

★

No, you don't get to be nice. I'm not going to play some stupid game with you where we act like we're friends and you get to walk out that door feeling good about yourself. I'm not a modern woman. If this is over, let's just call it over.

    —Mercedes Ruehl in *The Fisher King* (1991)

★

She was astonishing. So much so that I ended by falling on my knees and pledging her eternal love. And do you know that at that time and for several hours afterwards, I actually meant it.

—John Malkovich in *Dangerous Liaisons* (1988)

★

NICOLAS CAGE: I'm in love with you.
CHER: Snap out of it!
    —*Moonstruck* (1987)

★

SHIRLEY MACLAINE: I was curious. Do you have any reaction at all to my telling you I love you?

JACK NICHOLSON: I was just inches from a clean getaway.

    —*Terms of Endearment* (1983)

★

JACK NICHOLSON: I didn't know anybody old enough, so I thought, well, I'll ask my next-door neighbor. Well, anyway, they cancelled the dinner, but I was really thinking about asking you out, seriously. Isn't that a shocker?

SHIRLEY MACLAINE: Yes. Imagine you having a date with someone where it wasn't necessarily a felony.

    —*Terms of Endearment* (1983)

★

DIANE KEATON: I'm moving in with you, that's why.

WOODY ALLEN: Yeah, but you've got a nice apartment.

DK: I have a tiny apartment.

WA: I know it's small.

DK: That's right, and it's got bad plumbing and bugs.

WA: All right, granted, it has bad plumbing and bugs. But you say that like it's a negative thing. You know, entomology is a rapidly growing field.

    —*Annie Hall* (1977)

★

HUMPHREY BOGART: If that plane leaves the ground and you're not with him, you'll regret it—maybe not today, maybe not tomorrow, but soon, and for the rest of your life.

INGRID BERGMAN: But what about us?

HB: We'll always have Paris.

>   —*Casablanca* (1942)

★

ROY SCHEIDER: I say it a lot. A lot.

JESSICA LANGE: When?

RS: When it works.

>   —*All That Jazz* (1979)

★

You like to get hurt. Always picking the wrong guy. It's a sickness with a lot of women. Always looking for a new way to get hurt by a new man. Get smart. There hasn't been a new man since Adam.

>   —Richard Conte to Susan Hayward in *House of Strangers* (1949)

★

MERYL STREEP: You said you loved me.

DENNIS QUAID: I meant it at the time.

MS: What is it, a viral love? Kind of a twenty-four-hour thing?

>   —*Postcards From the Edge* (1990)

★

ISABEL JEANS: Did you notice that rope of black pearls around her throat?

LESLIE CARON: Oh yes, it was beautiful.

IJ: Dipped.

LC: Dipped?

IJ: Dipped. Given to her by the man she loves, whose love is obviously beginning to cool, and the poor thing doesn't know it. It's just a matter of time now.

    —*Gigi* (1958)

★

Your parent's place, my parent's place, your sister's apartment, the damn john at the pizza parlor. I'm telling ya Jo, I love you. Doesn't that mean anything to you? I think that when people love each other they should make a commitment. They should have a wedding in a church, with the blessing of God, for Chris'sakes. Don't ya get it, Jo? I'm telling you that I love you! And all you love is my dick.

    —Vincent Phillip D'Onofrio in *Mystic Pizza* (1988)

★

Did you happen to see that movie, *Unmarried Woman*? Well, I didn't get it. I mean, I would've been Mrs. Alan Bates so fast that guy wouldn't have known what hit him.

    —Goldie Hawn in *Private Benjamin* (1980)

★

That was a dead giveaway, you know, darling, wanting us to die together like that. Dying together is even more personal than living together.
  —Tallulah Bankhead in *Lifeboat* (1944)

★

Love means never having to say you're sorry.
  —Ali MacGraw to Ryan O'Neal in *Love Story* (1970)

★

That's the dumbest thing I ever heard.
  —Ryan O'Neal, responding to the same line from Barbra Streisand, in *What's Up, Doc?* (1972)

Proceed With the Execution

SIGOURNEY WEAVER: I think he's going to pop the question.

MELANIE GRIFFITH: You do?

SW: I think so. We're in the same city now. I've indicated that I'm receptive to an offer. I've cleared the month of June, and I am, after all, me.

   —*Working Girl* (1988)

★

Marry me, and I'll never look at any other horse.

   —Groucho Marx to Margaret Dumont in *A Day at the Races* (1937)

★

It's been a long time between offers. Kiss me. If that's all right, then everything else will be.

   —Sally Field, in response, in *Norma Rae* (1979)

★

With all the headaches ahead, you'll be my aspirin.

   —John Lund to Jean Arthur in *A Foreign Affair* (1948)

★

ELLEN BURSTYN: I scared your daddy into getting rich, beautiful.

CYBILL SHEPHERD: Well, if Daddy could do it, Duane could, too.

EB: Not married to you. You're not scary enough.

—*The Last Picture Show* (1971)

★

I'm in love with you. I love you. I am totally, completely mad for you. My heart stops every time I look at you. Personally, I think we should be married. I definitely want to have kids—four or five, if possible. There, I said it. It wasn't so difficult. You don't have to say anything. That's fine with me. I just wanted to get it out, myself. Talk about a load off.

—Al Pacino in *Frankie and Johnny* (1991)

★

JOHN MILJAN: I must have your golden hair, fascinating eyes, alluring smile, your lovely arms, your form divine—

MAE WEST: Wait a minute. Wait a minute! Is this a proposal, or are you taking inventory?

—*Belle of the Nineties* (1934)

★

I want us to put our teeth in the same glass at night.

—Burt Reynolds to Jill Clayburgh in *Starting Over* (1979)

★

You'll never want for food, and you'll never have to worry about rent. I've worked since I was seven. I've been a cabin boy, a seaman, a carpenter, a farmer, a miner, and a stevedore. I can give you numerous character references. I've good teeth. I'm…I'm not tattooed or nothing. I love you.

> —Richard Todd to Patricia Neal in *The Hasty Heart* (1950)

★

BETTY HUTTON: He was so sweet, honey. He said he loved me ever since I wasn't any bigger than a fire hydrant or something, and how he didn't blame me for not loving him because he was so homely in the face, and how he went to cooking class and sewing class just to be near me.

DIANA LYNN: But he's perfect. He could do all the housework!

> —*The Miracle of Morgan's Creek* (1944)

★

I don't owe a nickel in this town. I'll eat anything that's put down in front of me. I can fix anything electrical. I'm all right after my first cup of coffee—I want that bad, though. I got me a new job at the gas station, and I turn my paycheck over the minute I get it—that's every Friday. And I come straight home from work, and I stay there. I got me and Alice. We're alone. You got your two kids. You're alone. If you could help me, maybe I could help you.

> —Beau Bridges, proposing to Sally Field, in *Norma Rae* (1979)

★

Will you marry me? Did he leave you any money?
Answer the second question first.

    —Groucho Marx to Margaret Dumont in *Duck Soup*
    (1933)

★

In case you think I'm a fast worker, I've never told a woman I loved her or signed "Love" to a letter except to my folks. And I'm over thirty years old. Naturally, now that something's hit me, I can't waste any time.

> —James Broderick in *The Group* (1966)

★

Her father was very, very rich. And very, very sick. The doctors assured me he'd be dead any minute. There wasn't a second to lose. I rushed right out and married the boss's daughter.

> —Danny DeVito in *Ruthless People* (1986)

★

DANNY AIELLO: My mother is dying. When she's dead, I'll come back and we'll get married.

CHER: How near death is she?

> —*Moonstruck* (1987)

★

CHER: All right, the engagement is off!

DANNY AIELLO: In time, you will see that this is the best thing.

CHER: In time, you'll drop dead, and I'll come to your funeral in a red dress!

> —*Moonstruck* (1987)

★

I wasn't always rich. No, there was a time I didn't know where my next husband was coming from.

    —Mae West in *She Done Him Wrong* (1933)

★

I'll think it over, but I can tell ya now, the answer's no.

    —Judy Holliday to William Holden in *Born Yesterday* (1950)

★

JOE PESCI: I thought we'd get married this weekend.

MARISA TOMEI: You don't get it, do you? That is not romantic. I want a wedding in church, with bridesmaids and flowers.

JP: Whoa, whoa. How many times did you say that spontaneous is romantic?

MT: Hey, a burp is spontaneous. A burp is not romantic.

    —*My Cousin Vinny* (1992)

★

Jerry should never have died. I'd be better off. I could've divorced him.

    —Lily Tomlin in *9 to 5* (1980)

★

If you waited for a man to propose to you from natural causes, you'd die of old maidenhood.

    —Barbara Stanwyck in *The Lady Eve* (1941)

★

Why don't you get a divorce and settle down?
>—Oscar Levant to Joan Crawford in *Humoresque* (1946)

★

DANA IVEY: Why did I marry you?
DAN HEDAYA: Because I said yes.
>—*The Addams Family* (1991)

★

Garth, marriage is punishment for shoplifting, in some countries.
>—Mike Myers in *Wayne's World* (1992)

★

Listen, when I was courting your grandmother, it took me two years to propose. Know why? The moment she'd walk into a room, my knees would buckle, blood'd rush up into my head and…and the wall'd start to dance. Why, twice I keeled over in a dead faint…She finally dragged it out of me when I was in bed with a 104-fever—and in a state of hysteria. The moment she accepted, the fever went down to normal, and I hopped out of bed. Oh, the case was written up in all the medical journals as the phenomenon of the times. There was nothing phenomenal about it. I just had it bad, that's all. And I never got over it either.
>—Lionel Barrymore in *You Can't Take It With You* (1938)

★

I wanted to marry her when I saw the moonlight shining on the barrel of her father's shotgun.

> —Eddie Albert in *Oklahoma!* (1955)

★

Stand still, Godfrey. It'll all be over in a minute.

> —Carole Lombard to William Powell in *My Man Godfrey* (1936)

★

STEVE GUTTENBERG: I keep thinking I'm gonna be missing out on things, you know?

MICKEY ROURKE: Well, that's what marriage is all about.

> —*Diner* (1982)

★

NATALIE WOOD: I've got to do some thinking before I suddenly find myself married and settled down with children.

CLAIRE TREVOR: And what is so terrible about that? Some day you're going to have to do it.

> —*Marjorie Morningstar* (1958)

★

All you therapists ever want is for us to get married and have babies. It's the closest you'll ever get to a cure.

> —Meryl Streep in *Heartburn* (1986)

★

MAID: Don't you believe in marriage?

MARY CECIL: Sure I do—for women. But it's the sons of Adam that they gotta marry.

  —*The Women* (1939)

★

Now take it easy. There's nothing to be scared of. People do it every day. The bad part comes later.

  —Porter Hall (Justice of the Peace) in *The Miracle of Morgan's Creek* (1944)

★

I give 'em six months. Four if she cooks.

  —Dianne Wiest, on her daughter's marriage, in *Parenthood* (1989)

★

[Daughters are] a mess no matter how you look at 'em. A headache 'til they get married—*if* they get married—and, after that, they get worse. Either they leave their husbands and come back with four children and move into your guest room, or their husband loses his job and the whole *caboodle* comes back. Or else they're so homely you can't get rid of them at all, and they hang around the house like Spanish moss and shame you into an early grave.

  —William Demarest in *The Miracle of Morgan's Creek* (1944)

★

ALEC BALDWIN: Tess, will you marry me?

MELANIE GRIFFITH: Maybe.

AB: That's an answer?

MG: You want another answer, ask another girl.

　　—*Working Girl* (1988)

★

DARYL HANNAH: Are you speaking of our Lord? Is that Whose Name you're taking in vain?

KEVIN J. O'CONNOR: That's the one.

DH: Well, I am sorry, Sammy, but I am not about to spend the next fifty years of my life with someone who I'm not going to run into in the Hereafter.

　　—*Steel Magnolias* (1989)

★

Before a man gets married, he's like a tree in the forest. He stands there independent, an entity unto himself. And then he's chopped down. His branches are cut off, he's stripped of his bark, and he's thrown into the river with the rest of the logs. Then this tree is taken to the mill. And when it comes out, it's no longer a tree. It's the vanity table, the breakfast nook, the baby crib, and the newspaper that lights the family garbage can.

　　—Rock Hudson in *Pillow Talk* (1959)

★

Why did I cut myself off from every girl I know? Why does any man destroy himself? Because he thinks he's getting married!

—Rock Hudson in *Pillow Talk* (1959)

★

I just had the unpleasant sensation of hearing you referred to as my "husband."

—Claudette Colbert to Clark Gable in *It Happened One Night* (1934)

★

VINCENT GARDENIA: You did this once before. It didn't work out.

CHER: But the guy died.

VG: And what killed him?

C: He got hit by a bus.

VG: No, bad luck. Your mother and I were married fifty-two years, nobody died. You were married what, two years? Somebody's dead. Don't get married again, Loretta. It don't work out for you.

—*Moonstruck* (1987)

★

By the authority vested in me by Kaiser Wilhelm II, I pronounce you man and wife. Proceed with the execution.

—German captain to Katharine Hepburn and Humphrey Bogart in *The African Queen* (1952)

★

HELEN BRODERICK: Why did you two ever get married?
BARBARA STANWYCK: Ah, I don't know. It was raining and we were in Pittsburgh.
   —*The Bride Walks Out* (1936)

★

The responsibility for recording a marriage has always been up to the woman. If it wasn't for her, marriage would have disappeared long since. No man is going to jeopardize his present or poison his future with a lot of little brats hollering around the house unless he's forced to. It's up to the woman to knock him down, hogtie him, and drag him in front of two witnesses immediately, if not sooner. Anytime after that, it's too late.
   —Alan Bridge in *The Miracle of Morgan's Creek* (1944)

★

You know, I don't believe Clair has come right out and told me he loves me since we've been married. Of course, I know he does, because I keep reminding him of it. You have to keep reminding them.
   —Irene Dunne in *Life With Father* (1947)

★

I'm not living with you. We occupy the same cage, that's all.
   —Elizabeth Taylor to Paul Newman in *Cat on a Hot Tin Roof* (1958)

★

They all start out as Juliets and wind up as Lady Macbeths.
　　—William Holden in *The Country Girl* (1954)

★

Well, on to the slaughter!
　　—Elizabeth Taylor, before her wedding, in *Father of the Bride* (1950)

★

The new Medusa—my good wife.

> —Peter O'Toole re Katharine Hepburn in *The Lion in Winter* (1968)

★

Now he's gonna play that damn Vikki Carr record, and when he comes to bed he won't touch me.

> —Olympia Dukakis in *Moonstruck* (1987)

★

ELLEN BARKIN: You know, Elyse's mother is very upset with Eddie. You see, they picked out this yellow-and-white motif for the wedding. You know, like we did—napkins, tablecloths, bridesmaids, maid of honor, whole bit. Anyway, Eddie objected. He wanted blue and white—Colts' colors. Refused to give in.

DANIEL STERN: So?

EB: Well, you know how stubborn Eddie is.

DS: Could've been worse. Could've been black and gold—Steelers' colors.

> —*Diner* (1982)

★

I just couldn't go to Heaven without Clair. Why, I get lonesome for him even when I go to Ohio.

> —Irene Dunne re William Powell in *Life With Father* (1947)

★

LITTLE GIRL: Mommy, where is Daddy?

MOTHER: I don't know and I don't care. In the future you'll please refer
to him as "that heel"!

— *The Women* (1939)

★

That's the only good thing about divorce. You get to sleep with your
mother.

—Virginia Weidler, as Norma Shearer's daughter, in *The Women* (1939)

★

Listen, honey, don't you know that we dames have got to be a lot
more to the guy we marry than a schoolgirl sweetheart? We got to be a
wife—a real wife! And a mother, too, and a pal. Yeah, and a nursemaid.
Sometimes, when it comes to the point, we've even got to be a
"cutie." You should have licked that girl where she licked you—in his
arms. That's where you win in the first round. And, if I know men, it's
still Custer's Last Stand.

—Paulette Goddard in *The Women* (1939)

★

It's a pity that Leonardo da Vinci never had a wife to guide him. He
might have really gotten somewhere.

—William Holden in *The Country Girl* (1954)

★

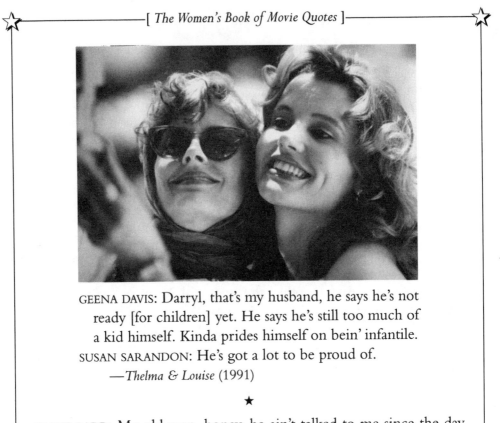

GEENA DAVIS: Darryl, that's my husband, he says he's not
   ready [for children] yet. He says he's still too much of
   a kid himself. Kinda prides himself on bein' infantile.
SUSAN SARANDON: He's got a lot to be proud of.
   —*Thelma & Louise* (1991)

★

DIANE LADD: My old man, honey, he ain't talked to me since the day
   Kennedy was shot.
ELLEN BURSTYN: Why, did he think you had something to do with it?
   —*Alice Doesn't Live Here Anymore* (1975)

★

It's funny. Susan and I do all the right things. We undress in front of each other, we spend fifteen minutes on foreplay. We experiment, do it in different rooms—it's a seven-room house. We don't believe in making a ritual of it. We do it when we feel like it. We don't feel we have to be passionate all the time. Sometimes it's even more fun necking. We're considerate of each other's feelings. I had a tendency—men, I guess, have—to be selfish. But I stopped. I don't do that now. We try to be patient, and we are—patient, gentle, with each other. Maybe it's just not meant to be enjoyable with women you love.

—Arthur Garfunkel in *Carnal Knowledge* (1971)

★

Who said anything about getting married? I feel that way about my girl because she *is* my girl. You'd never catch me feeling that way about a wife. Look Harvey, I've got a perfect setup. Why spoil it by getting married?

—Walter Matthau in *Cactus Flower* (1969)

★

All you have to do is give up a little bit of you for him. Don't make everything a game—just late at night in that little room upstairs. Take care of him. Make him feel important. If you can do that, you'll have a happy and wonderful marriage—like two out of every ten couples.

—Mildred Natwick to Jane Fonda in *Barefoot in the Park* (1967)

★

MADELINE KAHN: As the years go by, romance fades, and something else takes its place. Do you know what that is?
RYAN O'NEAL: Senility.
   —*What's Up, Doc?* (1972)

★

Martha, in my mind you are buried in cement right up to the neck. No, up to the nose. It's much quieter.
   —Richard Burton to Elizabeth Taylor in *Who's Afraid of Virginia Woolf?* (1966)

★

So we got married, ma'am. Naturally, I ain't had no chance to think about love since.
   —Marjorie Main in *The Women* (1939)

★

At the rate we've been having sex, we might as well be married already.
   —Geena Davis in *Earth Girls Are Easy* (1989)

★

EDWARD ALBERT: Sixteen! How long were you married?
GOLDIE HAWN: Oh God, it seemed like weeks.
   —*Butterflies Are Free* (1972)

★

I swear, if
you existed I'd
divorce you.
—Elizabeth Taylor
to Richard Burton
in *Who's Afraid of
Virginia Woolf?* (1966)

★

I believe that men grow old, and when sexual things no longer matter to them, they forget it all—forget what true passion is. If you ever felt what my son feels for your daughter, you've forgotten everything about it—my husband, too. You knew once, but that was a long time ago. Now the two of you don't know. And the strange thing for your wife and me is that you don't even remember.

    —Beah Richards to Spencer Tracy in *Guess Who's Coming to Dinner* (1967)

★

Ed hates anything that keeps him from going to the movies every night. I guess I'm what you call a Garbo widow.

    —Louise Closser Hale in *Dinner at Eight* (1933)

★

I thought it was for life, but the nice judge gave me a full pardon.

    —Katharine Hepburn, re her former marriage to Cary Grant, in *The Philadelphia Story* (1940)

★

Your father says that living apart without divorce is like living together without marriage. It just isn't respectable.

    —Polly Rowles in *The Group* (1966)

★

Marriage is like the Middle East. There's no solution.

    —Pauline Collins in *Shirley Valentine* (1989)

★

She tries to read my mind, and, if she can't read my mind, she reads my mail.

> —Walter Slezak on Ginger Rogers in *Once Upon a Honeymoon* (1942)

★

There's nothing out there for you, Jesse, except me in a different suit.
> —Burt Reynolds to Candice Bergen in *Starting Over* (1979)

★

That is a B, darling—the first letter of a seven-letter word that means your late father.

> —Rosalind Russell in *Auntie Mame* (1958)

★

Dave lost interest in me, and I lost interest in sex. I went shopping for gratification, but that's like sex without a climax.

> —Bette Midler in *Down and Out in Beverly Hills* (1986)

★

It's the normal people who are getting divorced. Nobody else even bothers to get married.

> —Jill Clayburgh in *An Unmarried Woman* (1978)

★

We came from mud. And after 3.8 billion years of evolution, at our core is still mud. Nobody can be a divorce lawyer and doubt that.

> —Danny DeVito in *The War of the Roses*

★

Losing a sweetheart is a private misfortune. Losing a wife is a public scandal.

—Clark Gable in *Possessed* (1931)

★

When you're dating, everything is talking about sex, right? Where can we do it, you know, why can't we do it? Are your parents going to be out so we can do it? Trying to get a weekend just so that we can do it. Everything is just always talking about getting sex. And then planning the wedding, all the details. But then, when you get married, you can get it whenever you want it. You wake up in the morning and she's there, and you come home from work and she's there. And so all that sex-planning talk is over with and so's the wedding-planning talk because you're already married. So—you know, I can come down here and we can bullshit the whole night away, but I cannot hold a five-minute conversation with Beth. I mean, it's not her fault. I'm not blaming her. She's great. It's just—it's just we got nothing to talk about.

—Daniel Stern in *Diner* (1982)

★

When a marriage goes on the rocks, the rocks are there [in bed]. Right there.

—Judith Anderson in *Cat on a Hot Tin Roof* (1958)

★

Hell Hath No Fury

JOBETH WILLIAMS: I know that Richard will always be faithful to me.
KEVIN KLINE: That's nice. A trust.
JW: No, fear of herpes.
>   —*The Big Chill* (1983)

★

The only way you could possibly redeem yourself, and be the man God intended you to be, is to admit to me anything that you might have been doing last night. Because if you don't do that, if you don't do that right now, you are a lost man. A shell. A bag of shit dust. You've gotta tell me. For us, honey.
>   —Debra Winger to Jeff Daniels in *Terms of Endearment* (1983)

★

When Arthur was having his little affair, every time he got on a plane I would imagine the plane crash, the funeral, what I would wear at the funeral. The flirting at the funeral. How soon I could start dating after the funeral.
>   —Stockard Channing in *Heartburn* (1986)

★

It's not necessarily that you fuck around—a lot. It's that you lie about it. You could have just told me the truth and then fucked them all. Have the cigarette with me.
—Meryl Streep in *Postcards From the Edge* (1990)

★

Stealing a man's wife, that's nothing. But stealing his car, that's larceny.
—John Garfield in *The Postman Always Rings Twice* (1946)

★

How American it is to want something better.
—Geraldine Brooks in *Possessed* (1947)

★

Well, you always have that blonde from Santa Barbara to fall back on—
if that's the phrase I'm looking for, and I think it probably is.
—Donna Mills to Clint Eastwood in *Play Misty for Me* (1971)

★

Get out. Go anywhere you want. Go to a hotel. Go live with her and
don't come back! Because after twenty-five years of building a home
and raising a family and all the senseless pain that we have inflicted on
each other, I'm damned if I'm going to stand here and have you tell
me you're in love with somebody else! Because this isn't a conventional
weekend with your secretary, is it? Or…or some broad that you picked
up after three belts of booze. This is your great winter romance, isn't
it? Your last roar of passion before you settle into your emeritus years.
Is that what's left for me? Is that my share? She gets the winter passion,
and I get the dotage? What am I supposed to do? Am I supposed to sit
at home knitting and purling while you slink back like some penitent
drunk? I'm your wife, damn it! And if you can't work up a winter passion for me, the least I require is respect and allegiance. I hurt! Don't
you understand that? I hurt badly!
—Beatrice Straight to William Holden in *Network* (1976)

★

Say, can you beat him? He almost stood me up for his wife!
—Joan Crawford in *The Women* (1939)

★

JASON BEGHE (state trooper at gunpoint): Please, I have a wife and kids.
GEENA DAVIS: You do? Well, you're lucky. You be sweet to 'em. Especially your wife. My husband wasn't sweet to me, and look how I turned out. Now go on. Get in [the car trunk].

    —*Thelma & Louise* (1991)

★

A relationship is a lot like a porcelain nail, Ted. You can break it and you can glue it back together, but it's not going to be as strong as it was unless the person is really committed and not bringing home nurses.

    —Geena Davis in *Earth Girls Are Easy* (1989)

★

What most wives fail to realize is that their husbands' philandering has nothing whatever to do with them.

    —John Halliday in *The Philadelphia Story* (1940)

★

I am not going to divorce you. I am going to forgive you. I am going to forget this ever happened. I'm going to figure out why it happened, and I'm never going to bring it up again as long as I live. And now, I'm going in there, and I'm going to spend every last cent you have.

    —Elaine May to Walter Matthau (husband) outside an expensive boutique in *California Suite* (1978)

★

It's getting late. I was beginning to worry. I was afraid you weren't in an accident.

—Jill Clayburgh to Burt Reynolds in *Starting Over* (1979)

★

MAURICE CHEVALIER: I was so much in love with you, I wanted to marry you. Yes, it's true. I was beginning to think of marriage. Imagine—marriage, me. Oh no, I was really desperate. I had to do something, and what I did was the soprano.

HERMIONE GINGOLD: Thank you, Honoré. That is the most charming and endearing excuse for infidelity that I have ever heard.

—*Gigi* (1958)

★

You want monogamy, marry a swan.

—Steven Hill in *Heartburn* (1986)

★

We women are so much more sensible. When we tire of ourselves, we change the way we do our hair, or hire a new cook, or, or decorate the house. I suppose a man could do over his office, but he never thinks of anything so simple. No, dear, a man has only one escape from his old self—to see a different self in the mirror of some woman's eyes.

—Lucile Watson to daughter Norma Shearer in *The Women* (1939)

★

A girl wouldn't be so bad. At least you could get teeth in a girl.
>—Elizabeth Taylor in *Father of the Bride* (1950)

★

A man hates to be told no woman but his wife is fool enough to love him.
>—Mary Cecil in *The Women* (1939)

★

Bad table manners, my dear Gigi, have broken up more households than infidelity.
>—Isabel Jeans to Leslie Caron in *Gigi* (1958)

★

JOHN MALKOVICH: Why do you suppose we only feel compelled to chase the ones who run away?
GLENN CLOSE: Immaturity?
>—*Dangerous Liaisons* (1988)

★

Do you still think men love the way we do? No, men enjoy the happiness they feel. We can only enjoy the happiness we give. They're not capable of devoting themselves exclusively to one person. So to hope to be made happy by love is a certain cause of grief.
>—Mildred Natwick in *Dangerous Liaisons* (1988)

★

It happens all the time on the road. He's gone for six months with a play, he gets lonely. The only time you have a good marriage is when your husband is in a flop. He's broke, but he's home.

—Marsha Mason in *The Goodbye Girl* (1977)

★

FRED MACMURRAY: You see a girl a couple of times a week, just for laughs, and right away they think you're going to divorce your wife. Now I ask you, is that fair?
JACK LEMMON: No sir, it's very unfair—especially to your wife.

—*The Apartment* (1960)

★

The first man that can think up a good explanation how he can be in love with his wife *and* another woman is going to win that prize they're always giving out in Sweden.

—Mary Cecil in *The Women* (1939)

★

It's very hard for a man to understand how a woman feels inside, although I tried to understand Frank—not that there's that much to understand. That's why I was so hurt when he strayed. But, you know me, Joan, I always try to look on the bright side. I just said to myself, "Well, at least she's the one who'll be nauseous now."

—Beatrice Arthur in *Lovers and Other Strangers* (1970)

★

I'm not going
to be ignored!
—Glenn Close
in *Fatal Attraction*
(1987)

LAURENCE HARVEY: Look, Gloria, I have to spend at least tonight with [my wife].

ELIZABETH TAYLOR: A good night's sleep will be the best thing for you.
  —*Butterfield 8* (1960)

★

How long does it take to tell a woman "My wife's come back"? I can say it in two seconds: "My wife's come back." You've had two days.
  —Irene Dunne to Cary Grant in *My Favorite Wife* (1940)

★

Pigs

BILLY CRYSTAL: This is a real classic by Mr. Pinsky. It's entitled *100 Girls I'd Like to Pork*.
RAYE BIRK: It's a coffee-table book.
—*Throw Momma From the Train* (1987)

★

I have no intention of breaking down her prejudices. I want her to believe in God and virtue and the sanctity of marriage, and still not be able to stop herself. I want the excitement of watching her betray everything that's most important to her.
—John Malkovich in *Dangerous Liaisons* (1988)

★

Use sincerity. It's the best technique.
—Joshua Cadman in *The Sure Thing* (1985)

★

Why can't women play the game properly? Everyone knows that in love affairs only the man has the right to lie.
—Clifton Webb in *Three Coins in the Fountain* (1954)

★

ANNETTE BENING: Hey, he didn't give you his big Walt Whitman speech, did he? The one about genius?

MERYL STREEP: I don't think so.

AB: Well, see, that's a good sign. That's his standard pickup line. That and the big Cambodian speech. Oh, and the thing about smelling like Catalina.

MS: *That* I've heard.

AB: Well, that's not bad. One out of three. You're obviously getting some new stuff, which means he must like you.

—*Postcards From the Edge* (1990)

★

ROY SCHEIDER: Goddamn it! How dare you use my phone, *my* telephone, to call somebody who's not gay?!

ANN REINKING: You can go out with any girl, any girl in town!

RS: That's right. I go out with any girl in town. I stay in with you.

—*All That Jazz* (1979)

★

Why do guys always know how to hit a woman—right across the cheek—wham—and it feels like your eye is going to explode. What do they do, do they pull you aside in high school and show you how to do this?

—Julia Roberts in *Pretty Woman* (1990)

★

Their dicks get limp when confronted by a woman of obvious power, and what do they do about it? Call them witches. Burn them. Torture them. Until every woman is afraid—afraid of herself, afraid of men, and all for what? Fear of losing their hard-on.

    —Jack Nicholson in *The Witches of Eastwick* (1987)

★

RICHARD GERE: Susan, tell me something. When you and I were dating, did you speak to my secretary more than you spoke to me?
JUDITH BALDWIN: She was one of my bridesmaids.

    —*Pretty Woman* (1990)

★

CARY GRANT: Since I have no intention of getting married, I feel honor-bound to declare myself at the beginning.
CECIL PARKER: What? Before the favor?
CG: Certainly before the favor. That's where the honor comes in. Now, how do I declare myself? By saying I never will marry? What woman really believes that? If anything, it's a challenge to them.
CP: Well, what do you do?
CG: Well, I say, "I *am* married. I'm married and I can't get a divorce." Now our position is clear. There can't be any misunderstanding later.

    —*Indiscreet* (1958)

★

I'm sorry, Louise. I seldom hit a woman, but if you don't leave me alone I'll wind up kicking babies.

—Van Heflin to Joan Crawford in *Possessed* (1947)

★

I thought all writers drank to excess and beat their wives. You know at one time I think I secretly wanted to be a writer.

—Cary Grant in *The Philadelphia Story* (1940)

★

See, when a girl's under twenty-one, she's protected by law. When she's over sixty-five, she's protected by nature. Anywhere in between, she's fair game.

—Cary Grant in *Operation Petticoat* (1959)

★

It's not as easy getting laid as it used to be. I don't think I fuck more than a dozen new girls a year now. Maybe I'm too much of a perfectionist. This last one came so close to being what I wanted. Good pair of tits on her—not a great pair. Almost no ass at all, and that bothered me. Sensational legs. I woulda settled for the legs if she had just two more inches here and three more here. Anyhow, that took two years outta my life.

—Jack Nicholson in *Carnal Knowledge* (1971)

★

JACK NICHOLSON: What kind of man am I?

RITA MORENO: A real man. A kind man.

JN: I'm not kind.

RM: I don't mean weak kind, the way so many men are. I mean the kindness that comes from enormous strength, from an inner power so strong that every act, no matter what, is more proof of that power. That's what all women resent. That's why they try to cut you down, because your knowledge of yourself is so right, so true, that it exposes the lies which they—every scheming one of them—live by. It takes a true woman to understand that the purest form of love is to love a man who denies himself to her, a man who inspires worship because he has no need for any woman. Because he has himself. And who is better, more beautiful, more powerful, more perfect—you're getting hard—more strong, more masculine, more extraordinary, more robust—it's rising, it's rising—more virile, more domineering, more irresistible—it's up. It's in the air!

—*Carnal Knowledge* (1971)

★

It's true! My brother told me. That's the way ladies are. They want you to try—even if they don't let you. Because even though they don't let you, they want you to.

—Jerry Houser in *Summer of '42* (1971)

★

CARY GRANT: I'll send the money right down to ya. I swear it on my mother's grave.

ROSALIND RUSSELL: All right, here's the sto—. Wait a minute, you're mother's alive!

　　—*His Girl Friday* (1940)

★

KATHARINE HEPBURN: You've got the mind of a pig.

CARY GRANT: It's a pig's world.

　　—*Sylvia Scarlett* (1935)

Goodbye, Baby

This picture is dedicated to all the beautiful women in the world who have shot their husbands full of holes out of pique.

>—Opening line of *Roxie Hart* (1942)

★

FRED MACMURRAY: Then there was the case of a guy who was found shot. His wife said he was cleaning a gun and his stomach got in the way. All she collected was a three-to-ten stretch in Tohatchapee.

BARBARA STANWYCK: Perhaps it was worth it to her.

>—*Double Indemnity* (1944)

★

SPENCER TRACY: Gladys, do you want me to kill myself?

JEAN HARLOW: Did you change your insurance?

>—*Libeled Lady* (1936)

★

KATHARINE HEPBURN: And after you shot him, how did you feel then?

JUDY HOLLIDAY: Hungry.

>—*Adam's Rib* (1949)

★

SUSAN SARANDON: But why would one of his women want to kill him?

JUDITH IVEY: Maybe he wouldn't go down on her.

SS: Don't you think murder is just a little bit excessive?

JI: I most certainly do not.

—*Compromising Positions* (1985)

★

You've got to have a sentimental reason for them to vote for you. Any decent actress can give a good performance. But a dying husband, that would've insured everything.

—Maggie Smith in *California Suite* (1978)

★

PETER O'TOOLE: Give me a little peace.

KATHARINE HEPBURN: A little? Why so modest? How about eternal peace?

—*The Lion in Winter* (1968)

★

GAILARD SARTAIN: What the hell's this?

KATHY BATES (his wife): That's a low-cholesterol meal.

GS: Are you trying to kill me?

KB: If I was going to kill you, I'd use my hands.

—*Fried Green Tomatoes* (1991)

★

Goodbye, baby.
     —Fred MacMurray, before shooting Barbara Stanwyck,
        in *Double Indemnity* (1944)

No matter where you go or what you do, you're gonna die.
> —Olympia Dukakis to Vincent Gardenia in *Moonstruck* (1987)

★

MARGARET DUMONT: My husband is dead.
GROUCHO MARX: I'll bet he's just using that as an excuse.
MD: I was with him to the end.
GM: No wonder he passed away.
MD: I held him in my arms and kissed him.
GM: So it was murder!
> —*Duck Soup* (1933)

★

Do I ice her? Do I marry her? Which one a dese?
> —Jack Nicholson re Kathleen Turner in *Prizzi's Honor* (1985)

★

WHOOPI GOLDBERG: This life be over soon. Heaven lasts always.
OPRAH WINFREY: Girl, you oughta bash Mister's head open and think about Heaven later.
> —*The Color Purple* (1985)

★

I need him like the ax needs the turkey.
> —Barbara Stanwyck in *The Lady Eve* (1941)

★

You have nothing to stay for. You have nothing to live for, really, have you? Look, down there—it's easy, isn't it? Why don't you? Why don't you? Go on. Go on. Don't be afraid.

> —Judith Anderson, trying to urge Joan Fontaine over a window ledge, in *Rebecca* (1940)

★

The doors made me do it.

> —Ida Lupino, confessing to asphyxiating her husband by closing the garage doors, in *They Drive by Night* (1940)

★

I loved you, Walter, and I hated him. But I wasn't going to do anything about it. Not until I met you. You planned the whole thing. I only wanted him dead.

>—Barbara Stanwyck to Fred MacMurray in *Double Indemnity* (1944)

★

Now, Sam. Do it now. Set me free. Set both of us free. He fell down the stairs and fractured his skull—that's how he died. Everybody knows what a heavy drinker he was. Oh Sam, it can be so easy.

>—Barbara Stanwyck, urging Van Heflin to kill husband Kirk Douglas in *The Strange Love of Martha Ivers* (1946)

★

Cancel my appointments.

>—A dying Sylvia Sidney in *Summer Wishes, Winter Dreams* (1973)

★

GEORGE BRENT: Judith, I want you to find peace. We all have to die. The tragic difference is that you know when and we don't. But the important thing is the same for all of us—to live our lives so that we can meet death whenever it comes, beautifully and finally.

BETTE DAVIS: Beautifully and finally. I'll die as I please. Now leave me alone!

>—*Dark Victory* (1939)

★

If anything happens to me, you tell every woman I've ever gone out with that I was talking about her at the end. That way they'll have to re-evaluate me.

—Albert Brooks in *Broadcast News* (1987)

★

Mothers

Sing out, Louise. Sing out!
   —Rosalind Russell in *Gypsy* (1962)

★

I refuse to endanger the health of my children in a house with less than four bathrooms!
   —Myrna Loy in *Mr. Blandings Builds His Dream House* (1948)

★

Dinner's gonna be late. Here boy! Here boy!
   —Judith Malina in *The Addams Family* (1991)

★

Give me a girl at an impressionable age, and she is mine for life.
   —Maggie Smith in *The Prime of Miss Jean Brodie* (1969)

★

I'm just your mother. You only owe me your entire existence on this planet. Please, Gordon, by all means, go sing, dance. DATE!
   —Elizabeth Wilson in *The Addams Family* (1991)

★

SHIRLEY MACLAINE: Emma, I'm totally convinced if you marry Flap Horton tomorrow it will be a mistake of such gigantic proportions it will ruin your life and make wretched your destiny.

DEBRA WINGER: Why are you doing this to me?

SM: You are not special enough to overcome a bad marriage.

 —*Terms of Endearment* (1983)

★

My mother didn't think that Leslie was suitable for a Vale of Boston. What man *is* suitable, Doctor? She's never found one! What man would look at me and say, "I want you"? I'm fat! My mother doesn't approve of dieting. Look at my shoes. My mother approves of sensible shoes. Look at the books on my shelves. My mother approves of good, solid books. I am my mother's well-loved daughter. I am her companion. I am my mother's servant. "My mother says." My mother, my mother, MY MOTHER!

 —Bette Davis in *Now, Voyager* (1942)

★

I think if you wear your glasses tonight, you'll be less of a shock to the others. And take off whatever you've got on your face. As to your hair and eyebrows, you can say that often after a severe illness one loses hair, but you're letting yours grow as quickly as possible.

 —Gladys Cooper to daughter Bette Davis in *Now, Voyager* (1942)

★

I'll never forget it. Never as long as I live. She said
"Mommy." And that was all.

> —Joan Crawford, after her daughter dies, in *Mildred
> Pierce* (1945)

When it comes to marriage, one man is as good as the next. And even the least accommodating is less trouble than a mother.

    —Glenn Close in *Dangerous Liaisons* (1988)

★

PIPER LAURIE: I can see your dirty pillows. Everyone will.
SISSY SPACEK: Breasts, Mama. They're called breasts.

    —*Carrie* (1976)

★

LONETTE MCKEE: Honey, you know what? Remember how we go to school in the morning and feed the pigeons and the squirrels? Remember the time the little bird was on the fence, the sparrow, and he was biting that other sparrow on the hooty? And the little squirrels with the penises were biting each other? Remember I said it was a spring thing? Mating season? Well, baby, that's what your mom and dad are doin'. We're making love.
VERONICA TIMBERS: I know. I was just testing if you would tell me the truth.

    —*Jungle Fever* (1991)

★

You know who I work for. My son is going to be all right. If not, I'll have you killed.

    —Anjelica Huston in *The Grifters* (1990)

★

ELLEN BURSTYN: I'm an okay sort of person. How did I get such a smart-ass kid?

ALFRED LUTTER (son): You got pregnant.

—*Alice Doesn't Live Here Anymore* (1975)

★

She told me she thinks I'm a son of a bitch. She also thinks I'm a funny son of a bitch. She loves me, but she doesn't like me. She's afraid of me, she's intimidated by me. She respects me, but she doesn't want to become like me. We have a perfectly normal mother-daughter relationship.

—Jane Fonda in *California Suite* (1978)

★

MERYL STREEP: Remember my seventeenth birthday party when you lifted your skirt in front of all those people?

SHIRLEY MACLAINE: I did not lift my skirt. It twirled up!

—*Postcards From the Edge* (1990)

★

SHIRLEY MACLAINE: How is she?

DOCTOR: I always tell people to hope for the best and prepare for the worst.

SM: And they let you get away with that?

—*Terms of Endearment* (1983)

★

MARA HOBEL: Yes, Mommie dearest.
FAYE DUNAWAY (as Joan Crawford): When I told you to call me that, I wanted you to mean it!
—*Mommie Dearest* (1981)

★

What if I do want them to amount to something? I'll do anything for those kids. Do you understand? Anything.

—Joan Crawford in *Mildred Pierce* (1945)

★

Sure would be nice to have a mother somebody liked.

—Debra Winger re Shirley MacLaine in *Terms of Endearment* (1983)

★

No wire hangaaaars!!!

—Faye Dunaway (as Joan Crawford) in *Mommie Dearest* (1981)

★

SHIRLEY MACLAINE: Every time I try to get close to you, you push me away. How would you like to have Joan Crawford for a mother? Or Lana Turner?
MERYL STREEP: These are the options?

—*Postcards From the Edge* (1990)

★

You're surprised. I insisted upon visiting the dead rabbit's grave.

—Ellen Burstyn in *Same Time, Next Year* (1978)

★

I *can't* have a baby, because I have a 12:30 lunch meeting!

—Diane Keaton in *Baby Boom* (1987)

★

Tell me, why is it doctors and nurses and husbands always seem to think they know more about this maternity business? Don't you think a mother learns anything in that little room they wheel 'em into, or is that just a kindergarten class? Let me tell you something: I picked up quite a little experience in that room, and it wasn't out of books, either.

    —Barbara Stanwyck in *Stella Dallas* (1937)

★

Personally, Veda's convinced me that alligators have the right idea. They eat their young.

    —Eve Arden in *Mildred Pierce* (1945)

★

A boy's best friend is his mother.

    —Anthony Perkins in *Psycho* (1960)

★

Had I been sterile, darling, I'd be happier today.

    —Katharine Hepburn to Anthony Hopkins, one of her English sons, in *The Lion in Winter* (1968)

★

I should've given you to God when you were born.

    —Piper Laurie to daughter Sissy Spacek in *Carrie* (1976)

★

Good, good Louis.
If I had managed
sons for him instead
of all those little
girls, I'd still be stuck
with being Queen
of France and we
should not have
known each other.
Such, my angels, is
the role of sex in
history.
—Katharine Hepburn
to her English sons in
The Lion in Winter
(1968)

★

You're an angel, honey. If your mother hadn't been such a bitch we coulda shared something important.

   —Bette Midler in *Beaches* (1988)

★

DIANE KEATON: They made some studies, I read in one of the psycho-analytic quarterlies. You don't need a male. I mean, two mothers are absolutely fine.

WOODY ALLEN: Really? Because I always feel very few people survive one mother.

   —*Manhattan* (1979)

★

TOM CRUISE: Some of the [prostitutes] are wearing my mother's clothing.

REBECCA DE MORNAY: So what's wrong with that?

TC: I just don't want to spend the rest of my life in analysis.

   —*Risky Business* (1983)

★

MERYL STREEP: Mom, I'm middle-aged.

SHIRLEY MACLAINE: *I'm* middle-aged.

MS: How many one-hundred-twenty-year-old women do you know?

   —*Postcards From the Edge* (1990)

★

Wednesday's great aunt Calpurnia— she was burned as a witch in 1706. They say she danced naked in the town square and enslaved a minister. Oh, yes. Don't worry. We've told Wednesday: college first.
—Anjelica Huston in *The Addams Family* (1991)

FAYE DUNAWAY: She's my daughter. [SLAP]

JACK NICHOLSON: I said I want the truth!

FD: She's my sister. [SLAP] She's my daughter. [SLAP] My sister, my daughter. [SLAP, SLAP]

JN: I said I want the truth!

FD: She's my sister *and* my daughter!

    —*Chinatown* (1974)

★

Well, there won't never be no patter of little feet in my house—unless I was to rent some mice.

    —Peggy Lee in *Pete Kelly's Blues* (1955)

★

You mustn't kid Mother, dear. I was a married woman before you were born.

    —Lucile Watson to Norma Shearer in *The Women* (1939)

★

Don't you think that everyone looks back on their childhood with a certain amount of bitterness and regret about something? It doesn't have to ruin your life, darling. You're a big girl now. Aren't you tired of it all? Bore, bore, bore! Life marches by, Chels. I suggest you get on with it.

    —Katharine Hepburn to Jane Fonda in *On Golden Pond* (1981)

★

No, no, no. I'm too young. You know, grandmothers are old. They bake and they sew and they tell you stories about the Depression. I was at Woodstock, for Chris'sake. I peed in a field! I've hung on to the Who's helicopter as it flew away!

—Dianne Wiest in *Parenthood* (1989)

★

Tell Mama. Tell Mama all.

—Elizabeth Taylor to Montgomery Clift in *A Place in the Sun* (1951)

★

Virtuosos

Well, that's it for tonight, folks. This is Sweet Sue, saying good night, reminding all you daddies out there that every girl in my band is a virtuoso—and I intend to keep it that way.

 —Joan Shawlee in *Some Like It Hot* (1959)

★

PATRICIA HITCHCOCK: She was a tramp.

LEO G. CARROLL: She was a human being. Let me remind you that even the most unworthy of us has the right to life and the pursuit of happiness.

PH: From what I hear, she pursued it in all directions.

 —*Strangers on a Train* (1951)

★

Going to a man's apartment always ends one of two ways. Either a girl's willing to lose her virtue, or she fights for it. I don't want to lose mine, and I think it's vulgar to fight for it, so I always put my cards on the table. Don't you think that's sensible?

 —Maggie McNamara to William Holden in *The Moon Is Blue* (1953)

★

It's not that I'm prudish. It's just that my mother told me never to enter any man's room in months ending in *r*.

>—Irene Dunne to Charles Boyer in *Love Affair* (1939)

★

NATALIE WOOD: What do I do about it?

CLAIRE TREVOR (mother): About what, darling?

NW: Oh, about the way I—feel sometimes.

CT: Take those feelings, put them in the bank, save them for the man who will appreciate them and love you for them after you marry him.

>—*Marjorie Morningstar* (1958)

★

Don't look so cross-eyed. It's not a fate worse than death. Listen, you take a poll of your graduating class 10 years from now, and just see how many of them clinched the deal without giving away a few free samples.

>—Carolyn Jones in *Marjorie Morningstar* (1958)

★

Henry was eighteen when we met, and I was Queen of France. He came down from the north to Paris with a mind like Aristotle's and a form like mortal sin. We shattered the Commandments on the spot.

>—Katharine Hepburn in *The Lion in Winter* (1968)

★

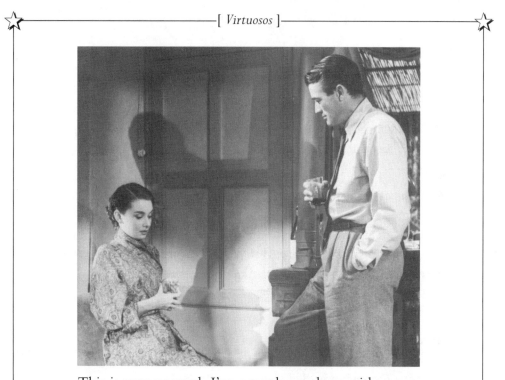

This is very unusual. I've never been alone with a man before—even with my dress on. With my dress off, it's *most* unusual.

> —Audrey Hepburn to Gregory Peck in *Roman Holiday* (1953)

★

GARY BROCKETTE: You a virgin?

CYBILL SHEPHERD: Yes, I am.

GB: Too bad.

CS: I don't want to be, though.

GB: I don't blame you. Come see me when you're not.

—*The Last Picture Show* (1971)

★

KATHARINE HEPBURN: Why? Was I so unattractive, so distant, so forbidding?

JAMES STEWART: You were extremely attractive, and as for distant and forbidding, on the contrary. But you also were a little the worse, or better, for wine, and there are rules about that.

—*The Philadelphia Story* (1940)

★

I'd never sleep with a player hittin' under .250. Well, unless he had a lot of RBIs or was a great glove man up the middle.

—Susan Sarandon in *Bull Durham* (1988)

★

Of course I may bring a boyfriend home occasionally, but only occasionally, because I do think that one ought to go to the man's room if one can. I mean, it doesn't look so much as if one expected it, does it?

—Liza Minnelli in *Cabaret* (1972)

★

You know, it takes two to get one in trouble.

—Mae West in *She Done Him Wrong* (1933)

★

UMA THURMAN: Are you saying I'm going to have to do *that* with three different men?

GLENN CLOSE: I'm saying, you stupid little girl, that provided you take a few elementary precautions, you can do it or not with as many men as you like, as often as you like, in as many different ways as you like. Our sex has few enough advantages. You may as well make the best of those you have.

—*Dangerous Liaisons* (1988)

★

That doesn't seem too offensive, as long as you're quiet. Chelsea always slept in the same bed with her husband. Ethel and I do, you know—we sleep together. Been doing it for years. No, I guess I'd be delighted to have you abuse my daughter under my own roof. Would you like the room where I first violated her mother?

—Henry Fonda to Dabney Coleman, his daughter's boyfriend, in *On Golden Pond* (1981)

★

If I'd have forgotten myself with that girl, I'd remember it.

—Fred Astaire in *Top Hat* (1935)

★

ANTHONY MESSURI (priest): What sins have you to confess?

CHER: Twice I took the name of the Lord in vain, once I slept with the brother of my fiancé, and once I bounced a check at the liquor store—but that was really an accident.

—*Moonstruck* (1987)

★

JOHN MALKOVICH: The countess has promised me extensive use of her gardens. It seems her husband's fingers are not as green as they once were.

GLENN CLOSE: Maybe not, but from what I hear, all his friends are gardeners.

—*Dangerous Liaisons* (1988)

★

She's like catnip to every cat in town.

—Tom Ahearne (bartender) re Elizabeth Taylor in *Butterfield 8* (1960)

★

EDDIE FISHER: What's with you and Yale? Always Yale.

ELIZABETH TAYLOR: It's the last college left.

EF: What?

ET: I started with Amherst, and I worked my way through the alphabet to Yale. I'm stuck there. Of course, I could work backwards again.

—*Butterfield 8* (1960)

★

She's got a traveling itch. She's like a flea—hop, hop, hop, from one dog to another. She bites you and she's gone. She picks you up and she drops you. Well, welcome to the fraternity. We meet once a year in Yankee Stadium.

> —Man in bar, re Elizabeth Taylor, in *Butterfield 8* (1960)

★

MADONNA: What if, at a key moment in the game, my uniform bursts open and—oops!—my bosoms come flyin' out. That might draw a crowd, right?

ROSIE O'DONNELL: You think there are men in this country who ain't seen your bosoms?

> —*A League of Their Own* (1992)

★

That is the kind of woman that makes whole civilizations topple.

> —Kathleen Howard (housekeeper) re Barbara Stanwyck in *Ball of Fire* (1942)

★

GLENN FORD: You can't talk to men down here the way you would at home. They don't understand it.

RITA HAYWORTH: Understand what?

GF: They think you mean it.

> —*Gilda* (1946)

★

Mama, face it! I was the slut of all time.
—Elizabeth Taylor in *Butterfield 8* (1960)

SUSAN HAYWARD: You're not my type.
JAMES PHILBROOK: I heard there was no such thing as "not your type."
 —*I Want to Live!* (1958)

★

If I'd been a ranch, they would have named me the Bar Nothing.
 —Rita Hayworth in *Gilda* (1946)

★

ANNETTE BENING: I'm Roy's friend.
ANJELICA HUSTON: Yes. I imagine you're lots of people's friend.
 —*The Grifters* (1990)

★

I have heard about your lunch breaks on the set. The only thing you don't do in your dressing room is dress.
 —Michael Caine to Maggie Smith in *California Suite* (1978)

★

Your idea of fidelity is not having more than one man in the bed at the same time. You're a whore, baby.
 —Dirk Bogarde to Julie Christie in *Darling* (1965)

★

When women go wrong, men go right after them.
 —Mae West in *She Done Him Wrong* (1933)

★

PAUL NEWMAN: You didn't, uh, offer him any encouragement by any chance, did you there, young lady?

WOMAN: No.

PN: That's funny. I was sittin' way over on the other side of the room, and *I* got a little bit encouraged.

—*Hud* (1963)

★

JAMES MASON: I want you to be my mistress. I've got it all drawn up. I proposed an agreement whereby either one of the contracting parties can opt out at any time in six-months' initial period. I bear all the expenses and undertake the formal adoption of the children. Here's a copy of the draft contract for your approval. I know it all looks pretty formal.

LYNN REDGRAVE: Um, will we have shareholders and things?

—*Georgy Girl* (1966)

★

JULIA ROBERTS: He's not really my uncle.

ELINOR DONAHUE: They never are, dear.

—*Pretty Woman* (1990)

★

It's so great to wake up in the morning with your rent paid.

—Julie Christie in *Shampoo* (1975)

★

WENDY MAKKENA: I'd rather sing than do anything. KATHY NAJIMY: It's better than ice cream. WM: It's better than springtime. WHOOPI GOLDBERG (posing as a nun): It's better than sex. No, no, I've *heard*.
—*Sister Act* (1992)

★

I mean, any gentleman with the slightest chic would give a girl a $50 bill for the powder room. And hold out for cab fare, too. That's another fifty.

—Audrey Hepburn in *Breakfast at Tiffany's* (1961)

★

MARILYN MONROE: Now there's something a girl could make sacrifices for…sable.

GREGORY RATOFF: Sable? Did you say sable or Gable?

MARILYN MONROE: Either one.

—*All About Eve* (1950)

★

JOAN CRAWFORD: Did you ever see a stenographer with a decent fur coat?

JOHN BARRYMORE: I have indeed.

JC: One she had bought herself?

—*Grand Hotel* (1932)

★

EMMA WALTON (fur protester): Do you know how many poor animals they had to kill to make that coat?

JOBETH WILLIAMS: Do you know how many rich animals I had to fuck to *get* this coat?

—*Switch* (1991)

★

Men have paid $200 for me, and here you are, turning down a freebie. You could get a perfectly good dish-washer for that.

—Jane Fonda to Donald Sutherland in *Klute* (1971)

The last time someone wanted to gag me, he tried it with a mink coat. But I went right ahead, and I never let go until the president of that particular ship company wound up in jail—even though I did get pneumonia that winter.

—Jean Arthur in *A Foreign Affair* (1948)

★

COAT CHECK GIRL: Goodness, what a beautiful diamond.
MAE WEST: Goodness had nothing to do with it, dearie.

—*Night After Night* (1932)

★

Remember, you're fighting for this woman's honor, which is probably more than she ever did.

—Groucho Marx re Margaret Dumont in *Duck Soup* (1933)

★

Command performances leave me quite cold. I've had more fun in the backseat of a '39 Ford than I could ever have in the vault of the Chase National Bank.

—Elizabeth Taylor in *Butterfield 8* (1960)

★

As long as they've got sidewalks, you've got a job.

—Joan Blondell to Claire Dodd in *Footlight Parade* (1933)

★

JEAN HARLOW: I was reading a book the other day.

MARIE DRESSLER: Reading a book!

JH: Yes. It's all about civilization or something—a nutty kind of book. Do you know that the guy said that machinery is going to take the place of every profession?

MD: Oh, my dear. That's something you need never worry about.

　　—*Dinner at Eight* (1933)

★

It doesn't matter who gives them as long as you never wear anything second-rate. Wait for the first-class jewels, Gigi. Hold on to your ideals.

　　—Isabel Jeans to Leslie Caron in *Gigi* (1958)

★

ANNE BAXTER: I'm afraid Mr. DeWitt would find me boring before too long.

MARILYN MONROE: You won't bore him, honey. You won't even get a chance to talk.

　　—*All About Eve* (1950)

★

ALAN FEINSTEIN: You are now a fallen woman.

DIANE KEATON: Thank God.

　　—*Looking for Mr. Goodbar* (1977)

★

So she said to herself, "You get in solid with the director, he puts you in solid with the producer, and pretty soon you wind up with a big part in the show." So two days—or should I say two nights—later, she was in but solid. Yeah, with the director, with his cousin. She was so busy being in solid with every Tom, Dick and Harry and his Uncle George, she wouldn't recognize a producer if she found one right under her pillow.

    —Kay Medford in *Butterfield 8* (1960)

★

I have seen women like you before—forty-six-year-old women who are still coquettes. They travel on boats often, always searching for something. Do you know where that searching ends, Miss Treadwell? It ends by sitting in a nightclub with a paid escort who tells you the lies you must hear.

    —Werner Klemperer to Vivien Leigh in *Ship of Fools* (1965)

★

Look, with these gals that want to buy it, most of 'em are old and dignified—social-register types, you know what I mean? They can't be trottin' down to Times Square to pick out the merchandise.

    —Dustin Hoffman in *Midnight Cowboy* (1969)

★

Are We All Lit?

BETTE DAVIS: *Encore du champagne.*
WAITER: More champagne, Miss Channing?
BD: That's what I said, bub.
    —*All About Eve* (1950)

★

There comes a time in every woman's life when the only thing that helps is a glass of champagne.

    —Bette Davis in *Old Acquaintance* (1943)

★

I always start [drinking] around noon—in case it gets dark early.

    —Peggy Lee in *Pete Kelly's Blues* (1955)

★

Get me a bromide. And put some gin in it.

    —Mary Boland in *The Women* (1939)

★

Gimmer visky…ginger ale on the side. And don't be stingy, baby.

    —Greta Garbo in *Anna Christie* (1930)

★

My, you are making me thirsty just standing there. Now you can open the champagne. Pour me a drink. And set the bottle down.

    —Carole Cook, a client, to Richard Gere in *American Gigolo* (1980)

★

I'll admit I may have seen better days, but I'm still not to be had for the price of a cocktail, like a salted peanut.

    —Bette Davis in *All About Eve* (1950)

★

LUCILLE BALL: Could you be persuaded to have a drink, dear?

BEATRICE ARTHUR: Well, maybe just a tiny triple.
—*Mame* (1974)

★

There now, are we all lit?
>—Rosalind Russell in *Auntie Mame* (1958)

★

Of all the gin joints in all the towns in all the world, she walks into mine.
>—Humphrey Bogart in *Casablanca* (1942)

★

Martha? Rubbing alcohol for you?
>—Richard Burton to Elizabeth Taylor in *Who's Afraid of Virginia Woolf?* (1966)

★

Please, darling, your Auntie Mame is hung!
>—Rosalind Russell in *Auntie Mame* (1958)

★

You Tell Me

MARK LAMOS: No, he's straight. I asked.

MARY-LOUISE PARKER: Well, he lives with another guy, and they both have great bodies. You tell me.

    —*Longtime Companion* (1990)

★

Don't you know they have a secret language? You go on, ask him if he has a pair of alligator shoes. I'll lay ya five-to-one he'll jump right on your bones.

    —Liza Minnelli in *The Sterile Cuckoo* (1969)

★

MAGGIE SMITH: Why do you stay with me? What do you get from me that could possibly satisfy you?

MICHAEL CAINE: A wider circle of prospects.

    —*California Suite* (1978)

★

Obviously, those three girls were just the wrong three girls!

    —Liza Minnelli in *Cabaret* (1972)

★

ROCK HUDSON: There are some men who just are very
   devoted to their mothers. You know, the type that
   likes to collect cooking recipes, or exchange bits of
   gossip.
DORIS DAY: What a vicious thing to say!
   —*Pillow Talk* (1959)

In my day you could tell by a man's carriage and demeanor which side his bread was buttered on. But in this day and age, who knows? I asked Marshall, "How can you tell?" And he said, "All gay men have track lightin', and all gay men are named Mark, Rick, or Steve."

    —Olympia Dukakis in *Steel Magnolias* (1989)

★

Oh, Miss Mann, I can't believe I'm meeting you. Ever since I was about seven I wanted to be you.

    —Young man to Shirley MacLaine in *Postcards From the Edge* (1990)

★

JULIE ANDREWS: How long have you been a homosexual?
ROBERT PRESTON: How long have you been a soprano?
JA: Since I was twelve.
RP: I was a late bloomer.

    —*Victor/Victoria* (1982)

★

DUSTIN HOFFMAN: She thinks I'm gay....
SYDNEY POLLACK: Well, sleep with her, and she'll know you're not.
DH: I slept with her once. She still thinks I'm gay.
SP: Oh. That's not so good, Michael.

    —*Tootsie* (1982)

★

JOHN CUSACK: You told her I was a virgin?

ANTHONY EDWARDS: So I exaggerated a little. Girls like virgins. They find them a challenge.

JC: You told her I was gay!

AE: It's a bigger challenge.

    —*The Sure Thing* (1985)

★

OLYMPIA DUKAKIS: Since when do you have track lightin'?

SHIRLEY MACLAINE: 'Bout three weeks. It's in the foyer up the staircase. My grandson's idea.

JULIA ROBERTS: I haven't seen him in ages. How is he?

SM: Steve's fine.

    —*Steel Magnolias* (1989)

★

CHRIS MCDONALD: I want to be with you.

SHELLEY LONG: That's nice. This is so funny, George. I thought you were gay.

CM: I am. It's just that I play so many heterosexual roles, I feel I really need to do some serious research.

    —*Outrageous Fortune* (1987)

★

TONY CURTIS: Jerry, you can't be serious.

JACK LEMMON: Why not? He keeps marrying girls all the time.

TC: But you're not a girl. You're a guy, and why would a guy want to marry a guy?

JL: Security.

—*Some Like It Hot* (1959)

★

MICHAEL YORK: Screw Maximillian!

LIZA MINNELLI: I do.

MY: So do I.

  —*Cabaret* (1972)

★

LIZA MINNELLI: Well, do you sleep with girls or don't you?
MICHAEL YORK: Sally, you don't ask questions like that.
LM: I do.

    —*Cabaret* (1972)

★

Vive la Difference!

Do you think God knew what he was doing when he created woman? Huh? No shit, I really want to know. Or do you think it was just another one of His minor mistakes, like tidal waves? Earthquakes? Floods!

> —Jack Nicholson in *The Witches of Eastwick* (1987)

★

I'd love to be a woman.

> —Jack Nicholson in *The Witches of Eastwick* (1987)

★

Queen Cleopatra is widely read, well versed in the natural sciences and mathematics. She speaks seven languages proficiently. Were she not a woman, one would consider her to be an intellectual.

> —Andrew Keir, re Elizabeth Taylor in *Cleopatra* (1963)

★

I've never seen a woman who was more a man. She thinks like one, acts like one, and sometimes makes me feel like I'm not.

> —Cowboy, re Joan Crawford in *Johnny Guitar* (1954)

★

KATHARINE HEPBURN: Well, maybe there is a difference, but it's a little difference.

SPENCER TRACY: Well, you know, as the French say, "Vive la difference!"

KH: Which means?

ST: Which means hurray for that little difference.

    —*Adam's Rib* (1949)

★

Women today are better hung than the men.

>—Jack Nicholson in *Carnal Knowledge* (1971)

★

I wouldn't mind losing like a man if you weren't so damned determined to win like one.

>—Dudley Moore to Julie Andrews in *"10"* (1979)

★

Women are obliged to be far more skillful than men. You can ruin our reputation and our life with a few well-chosen words. So of course I had to invent not only myself, but ways of escape no one has ever thought of before. And I've succeeded because I've always known I was born to dominate your sex and avenge my own.

>—Glenn Close in *Dangerous Liaisons* (1988)

★

She shouldn't try to be top man. She's not built for it. She's flying in the face of nature.

>—Ray Milland re Ginger Rogers in *Lady in the Dark* (1944)

★

I had lunch with Karen not three hours ago. As always with women who try to find out things, she told more than she learned.

>—George Sanders in *All About Eve* (1950)

★

Now you listen to me. I don't know Rosie but I know women. Some of my best friends are women.

—Tallulah Bankhead in *Lifeboat* (1944)

★

SHELLEY LONG: You're calling my Hamlet a wimp?

BETTE MIDLER: He's a wimp. I mean, look at him. He can't make up his mind about anything. He stands around all night and says, "What'll I do? What'll I do? What'll I do?" Give me Romeo or Henry V—now there's a guy I could boff.

—*Outrageous Fortune* (1987)

★

Look at that! Look how she moves! That's just like Jell-O on springs. She must have some sort of built-in motor or something, huh? I tell you it's a whole different sex.

—Jack Lemmon re Marilyn Monroe in *Some Like It Hot* (1959)

★

SAILOR: Quit talkin' about her that way. She's a woman!

SAILOR #2: So?

S: Well, my mother's a woman.

S #2: So?

S: I don't know. It just all seems to tie in somehow.

—*Operation Petticoat* (1959)

★

ALAN ALDA: No.
JANE FONDA: No what?
ALAN ALDA: No sir.
    —*California Suite* (1978)

★

You boys stopped fightin'? Pals now? That's good. I love a little macho male bondin'. I think it's sweet. I do. Even if it probably is latent homosexuality bein' rechanneled. I'm all for rechannelin', so who cares, right?

    —Susan Sarandon in *Bull Durham* (1988)

★

That's what my ex-wife used to keep reminding me of, tearfully. She had a theory that behind every great man there was a great woman. She also was thoroughly convinced that she was great. And that all I needed to qualify was guidance on her part. She worked hard at it. Too hard.

    —William Holden in *The Country Girl* (1954)

★

Don't confide in your girlfriends…. If you let them advise you, they'll see to it in the name of friendship that you lose your husband and your home. I'm an old woman, my dear. I know my sex.

    —Lucile Watson in *The Women* (1939)

★

WILLIAM HOLDEN: Why is it that women always think they understand men better than men do?

GRACE KELLY: Maybe because they live with them.

    —*The Country Girl* (1954)

★

Women! They get stirred up, and then they try to get you stirred up, too. But don't you let them do it, Clarence. Don't you let them do it. Now if you can keep reason and logic in the argument—well, a man can hold his own, of course. But if they can switch you, pretty soon the argument's about whether you love them or not. I swear I don't know how they do it. But don't you let them, Clarence. Don't you let them.

    —William Powell to his son in *Life With Father* (1947)

★

ROSIE PEREZ: It's a way of controlling a woman.

WOODY HARRELSON: Bringing 'em a glass of water?

RP: Yes. I read it in a magazine. See, if I'm thirsty, I don't want you to bring me a glass of water. I want you to sympathize. I want you to say "Gloria, I too know what it feels like to be thirsty. I too have had a dry mouth." I want you to connect with me, through sharing and understanding, the concept of dry-mouthedness.

    —*White Men Can't Jump* (1992)

★

There is no sincerity like a woman telling a lie.
> —Cecil Parker re Ingrid Bergman in *Indiscreet* (1958)

★

I know he's a good man. You know he's a good man. My bad days are when *he* knows he's a good man.
> —Katharine Hepburn re Spencer Tracy in *State of the Union* (1948)

★

Only time a woman doesn't care to talk is when she's dead.
> —William Demarest in *The Miracle of Morgan's Creek* (1944)

★

With most fellas, if you say something like "My favorite season's autumn," they go "Oh, my favorite season's spring." And then they go ten minutes talking about why they like spring. And you ain't talking about spring. You're talking about autumn. So what do you do? Talk about what they want to talk about, or you don't talk at all. Or you wind up talking to yourself.
> —Pauline Collins in *Shirley Valentine* (1989)

★

We men are pretty much alike. You see, we like to think we stand alone, but there's generally a woman standing beside us.
> —Clark Gable in *Possessed* (1931)

★

Listen to the woman very carefully. Women know shit. I mean, even if you don't get the words, even if you don't know what the hell she's talking about, just listen.

—Wesley Snipes in *White Men Can't Jump* (1992)

★

ADOLPHE MENJOU: You're the most beautiful plank in your husband's platform.

KATHARINE HEPBURN: That's a heck of a thing to call a woman!

—*State of the Union* (1948)

★

You've got no faith in Johnny, have you, Julia? His little dream may fall flat, you think. Well, so it may! What if it should? There'll be another. Oh, I've got all the faith in the world in Johnny. Whatever he does is all right with me. If he wants to dream for a while, he can dream for a while. And if he wants to come back and sell peanuts—oh, how I'll believe in those peanuts!

—Katharine Hepburn in *Holiday* (1938)

★

Listen to me, mister. You're my knight in shining armor. Don't you forget it. You're going to get back on that horse, and I'm going to be right behind you, holding on tight, and away we're gonna go, go, go!

—Katharine Hepburn to Henry Fonda in *On Golden Pond* (1981)

★

Sacrifice is dated, Mother. You don't reform a man. He only drags you down.

> —Joan Hackett in *The Group* (1966)

★

NORMA SHEARER: Talk to me all you want, but what does it come down to? Compromise.

PAULETTE GODDARD: Well, what the heck, a woman's compromised the day she's born.

> —*The Women* (1939)

★

I was a better man with you, as a woman, than I ever was with a woman, as a man. Know what I mean? I just gotta learn to do it without the dress.

—Dustin Hoffman to Jessica Lange in *Tootsie* (1982)

★

That cynicism you refer to I acquired the day I discovered I was different from little boys.

—Celeste Holm in *All About Eve* (1950)

★

Your love affair with yourself has reached heroic proportions. It doesn't seem to leave much room for me. Are you sure you can get along without somebody to help you admire yourself?

—Joan Crawford to Van Heflin in *Possessed* (1947)

★

Believe you me, if it didn't take men to make babies, I wouldn't have anything to do with any of you!

—Gena Rowlands to Kirk Douglas in *Lonely Are the Brave* (1962)

★

Oh, men! I never yet met one of them who didn't have the instincts of a heel. Sometimes I wish I could get along without them.

—Eve Arden in *Mildred Pierce* (1945)

★

God took a rib from Adam and made Eve. Now maybe men chase women to get the rib back.

    —Danny Aiello in *Moonstruck* (1987)

★

You use men to meet other men.

    —Jessica Walter in *The Group* (1966)

★

I think man was made in the devil's image and women were created out of God. 'Cause after all, women can have babies, which is kind of like creating. And which also accounts for the fact that women are so attracted to men. 'Cause let's face it, the devil is a hell of a lot more interesting. I slept with some saints in my day. Believe me, I know what I'm talking about.

    —Mercedes Ruehl in *The Fisher King* (1991)

★

STEVE MARTIN: That's the difference between men and women. Women have choices, men have responsibilities.

MARY STEENBURGEN: Oh, really. Oh, okay. Well then, I choose for you to have the baby, Okay? That's my choice. You have the baby, you get fat, you breast-feed 'til your nipples are sore. I'll go back to work.

    —*Parenthood* (1989)

★

CHER: I don't think that men are the answer to everything.

MICHELLE PFEIFFER: No.

SUSAN SARANDON: Then why do we always end up
talking about them?
—*The Witches of Eastwick* (1987)

★

Balls, said the queen. If I had 'em, I'd be king.
—Jill Clayburgh in *An Unmarried Woman* (1978)

★

The only difference in men is the color of their neckties.
—Helen Broderick in *Top Hat* (1935)

★

You're the first woman I've seen at one of these things that dresses like a woman, not like a woman thinks a man would dress if he was a woman.

—Harrison Ford to Melanie Griffith in *Working Girl* (1988)

★

You can help with the dishes, even though it's not a man-type thing to do. Man-type things, woman-type things. What does the creative force behind the universe care about such foolishness?

—Diane Ladd to Robert Duvall in *Rambling Rose* (1991)

★

Bill's thirty-two. He looks thirty-two. He looked it five years ago, he'll look it twenty years from now. I hate men.

—Bette Davis in *All About Eve* (1950)

★

Really there's no difference between grown men and little boys. It's the same as it was in the sandbox—except for then they wanted to pull your panties down in public.

—Andie MacDowell in *The Object of Beauty* (1991)

★

Men don't get smarter when they grow older. They just lose their hair.

—Claudette Colbert in *The Palm Beach Story* (1942)

★

Men's all alike, married or single. It's their game.
    —Mae West in *She Done Him Wrong* (1933)

★

You poor guys. Always confusing your pistols with your privates.
    —Michelle Pfeiffer in *Batman Returns* (1992)

★

Screen Gems

Oh, Jerry, don't let's ask for the moon—we have the stars.
>—Bette Davis in *Now, Voyager* (1942)

★

What a dump.
>—Bette Davis in *Beyond the Forest* (1949)

★

CELESTE HOLM: Margot, nothing you've ever done has made me as happy as your taking Eve in.
BETTE DAVIS: I'm so happy you're happy.
>—*All About Eve* (1950)

★

It took more than one man to change my name to Shanghai Lily.
>—Marlene Dietrich in *Shanghai Express* (1932)

★

I want to be alone.
>—Greta Garbo in *Grand Hotel* (1932)

★

JOAN CRAWFORD: You wouldn't be able to do these awful things to me if I weren't still in this [wheel] chair.
BETTE DAVIS: But cha are, Blanche! Ya *are* in that chair!
—*What Ever Happened to Baby Jane?* (1962)

★

Suddenly, you're afraid, and you don't know what you're afraid of. Did you ever get that feeling?… Well, when I get it, the only thing that does any good is to jump into a cab and go to Tiffany's. Calms me down right away. The quietness and the proud look of it. Nothing very bad could happen to you there.

—Audrey Hepburn in *Breakfast at Tiffany's* (1961)

★

La-di-da.

—Diane Keaton in *Annie Hall* (1977)

★

Fiddle-de-dee!

—Vivien Leigh in *Gone With the Wind* (1939)

★

As God is my witness, they're not going to lick me. I'm going to live through this, and when it's all over, I'll never be hungry again—no, nor any of my folk. If I have to lie, steal, cheat, or kill, as God is my witness, I'll never be hungry again!

—Vivien Leigh in *Gone With the Wind* (1939)

★

No one ever leaves a star. That's what makes one a star.

—Gloria Swanson in *Sunset Boulevard* (1950)

★

I always get the fuzzy end of the lollipop.
—Marilyn Monroe in *Some Like It Hot* (1959)

Does this boat go to Europe, France?

> —Marilyn Monroe in *Gentlemen Prefer Blondes* (1953)

★

VIVIEN LEIGH: Rhett, if you go, where shall I go? What shall I do?
CLARK GABLE: Frankly, my dear, I don't give a damn.

> —*Gone With the Wind* (1939)

★

Tara! Home. I'll go home. I'll think of some way to get him back. After all, tomorrow is another day!

> —Vivien Leigh's final lines in *Gone With the Wind* (1939)

★

Toto, we're home! Home. And this is my room. And you're all here. And I'm not going to leave here ever, ever again. Because I love you all, and, oh Auntie Em, there's no place like home!

> —Judy Garland's final lines in *The Wizard of Oz* (1939)

★

Toto, too!

> —Billie Burke in *The Wizard of Oz* (1939)

★

Toto, I have a feeling we're not in Kansas anymore.

> —Judy Garland in *The Wizard of Oz* (1939)

★

I'll get you, my pretty. And your little dog, too!
—Margaret Hamilton in *The Wizard of Oz* (1939)

★

The calla lilies are in bloom again. Such a strange flower, suitable to any occasion. I carried them on my wedding day, and now I place them here in memory of something that has died.

—Katharine Hepburn in *Stage Door* (1937)

★

If we bring a little joy into your humdrum lives, it makes us feel our work ain't been in vain for nothin'.

—Jean Hagen in *Singin' in the Rain* (1952)

★

Hello, everybody. This is Mrs. Norman Maine.

—Judy Garland in *A Star Is Born* (1954), also Janet Gaynor (1937)

★

Life is a banquet, and most poor suckers are starving to death!

—Rosalind Russell in *Auntie Mame* (1958)

★

There was a time in this business when they had the eyes of the whole wide world. But that wasn't good enough for them. Oh, no. They had to have the ears of the world, too. So they opened their big mouths and out came talk, talk, talk!

—Gloria Swanson in *Sunset Boulevard* (1950)

★

WILLIAM HOLDEN: You're Norma Desmond! You used to be in silent pictures. Used to be big.

GLORIA SWANSON: I am big. It's the pictures that got small.

—*Sunset Boulevard* (1950)

★

Play it, Sam. Play "As Time Goes by.'"
    —Ingrid Bergman to Dooley Wilson in *Casablanca* (1942)

★

You see, this is my life. It always will be. There's nothing else. Just us, and the cameras, and those wonderful people out there in the dark. All right, Mr. DeMille. I'm ready for my close-up.
    —Gloria Swanson in *Sunset Boulevard* (1950)

★

Actress and Actor Index

Movie Index